# QUENTIN
# TARANTINO

## THE ICONIC FILMMAKER AND HIS WORK

First published in 2019 by White Lion Publishing,
an imprint of The Quarto Group.
1 Triptych Place, 2nd Floor
London, SE1 9SH,
United Kingdom
T (0)20 7700 6700
www.quarto.com

A catalogue record for this book is available from the British Library.

ISBN  978 1 78131 775 4
Ebook ISBN 978 1 78131 868 3

10

Designed by Sue Pressley and Paul Turner, Stonecastle Graphics Ltd

Printed in China

# QUENTIN
# TARANTINO

## THE ICONIC FILMMAKER AND HIS WORK

Ian Nathan

WHITE LION PUBLISHING

# CONTENTS

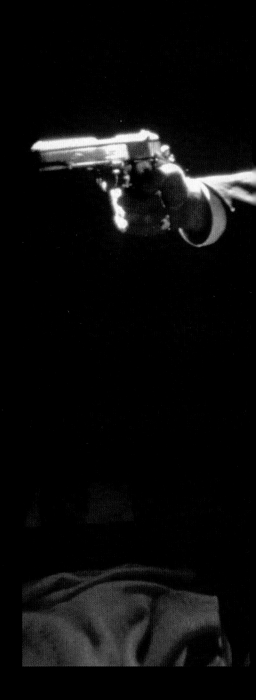

**Above:** John Travolta and Samuel L. Jackson in *Pulp Fiction*, featuring
Los Angeles mobsters and a mysterious briefcase.

# INTRODUCTION

## 'The heartbeat of a movie has to be a human heartbeat ...' *Quentin Tarantino* [1]

It was towards the end of the summer of 1995 when the British press finally got to see the Second Film by Quentin Tarantino. That was when we finally understood what we were dealing with. We had all heard the rumours, of course; there was no missing the hoopla that had surrounded the former video store clerk's triumph at Cannes the previous spring.

Honestly, we were up to speed on the Tarantino phenomenon taking shape on either side of the Atlantic. I had attended the notorious London Film Festival screening of *Reservoir Dogs* two years earlier, where a noticeable portion of the audience had upped and left, their lips pursed in disgust as Mr. Blonde unsheathed his razor. The rest of us had remained, glued to our seats, horrified and enthralled.

*Reservoir Dogs* was quite something, we all agreed. But I have never been to a screening like the night they showed *Pulp Fiction* in London. This wasn't the hushed decorum of cinemagoing, this was the adrenalin surge of a rock concert, the inexorable climb and plunge of a rollercoaster, or the snap of a hard drug. It was like a wild frat-house initiation (into Alpha Geek, which began as Amanda Plummer began waving her gun around like a lunatic, followed by the heady wave of Dick Dale and his Del-Tones's surf guitars on 'Misirlou' (the score remained imperious and giddy throughout). It was if we had been plugged into the mains. The applause was spontaneous.

By the time  Vincent (in John Travolta's touchingly terrified hands) readied himself to spear Mia Wallace (Uma Thurman, her pale face smeared with blood and heroin snot) with a hypodermic that could have impaled rhino hide, there was genuine screaming: terrified, awed, thrilled not by special effects but by this mix of dread and humour. We were laughing for our lives.

That night, as we left, it felt as if we had woken up.

From the very first, and the very second, and ever since, Tarantino has remained an artist operating entirely on his own terms. He couldn't turn out a routine piece of craftsmanship if he had a gun to his head.

**Above:** Quentin Tarantino in conversation with Harvey Keitel during the shoot for *Reservoir Dogs*. While it was his very first film, Tarantino was never intimidated about working with such strong personalities. An ironclad belief in his gifts as filmmaker seemed to be written into his DNA.

He could only ever be Quentin Tarantino, bidden by his talkative characters.

His story became gospel. Overnight from the counter of an outré video store in Manhattan Beach, California where he argued on behalf of cult classics and European auteurs to the most dynamic new voice to hit cinema since Martin Scorsese. Of course, it was a whole lot more complicated and interesting than that, but you get the gist. Here was a glimpse of possibility for every hopeful outsider.

That is key to the Tarantino myth – the optimism that accompanied him. He was the messiah of film geeks.

His is a voice made from movies. Has he seen every movie ever made? Maybe not quite, but he must have come close. Celluloid runs through his veins, slice him with a razor blade and he will bleed movies. *The Good, The Bad and The Ugly* remains his all-time favourite (for now), but he is open to all-comers, able to find as many rewards in the scuzziest drive-in shocker as any arthouse darling.

Thankfully, he has outlasted his own cult, matured, but never compromised. His eighth and latest, *The Hateful Eight* (2015), stands amongst his best. He is a paradox that Hollywood still can't fathom. A marriage made of art and commerce; trash and humanity; violence and laughter. These are stories that ride high on their own artifice, yet feel real. His gift is to fuse the illusions of cinema with the rhythms of life to see what comes of it.

Warping beloved genres has always been his way into a story, and his canon has covered crime, horror, Western and war movies (and subdivisions thereof). Truly, though, these are films about human folly, and what binds and separates us; about communication, language, violence, race, underworld ethics and righteous fury; about reinventing form and dancing with time; and that singular conundrum known as America.

Unlike so many other filmmakers who struggle to elaborate their creative process, in interview Tarantino is hyper-articulate. With every answer to every question it sounds like he is quoting from a biography already written in his head. There is no one better on Tarantino than Tarantino. Here is an ego like a tumbling waterfall, and with a drive to match.

Beware, though, he is a self-mythologizer too, which is all part of the fun. This book is not only a celebration of his career but an attempt to decipher the fire-hydrant spills of those answers, and all the inspirations and connections that marry and separate his still relatively compact output.

What is incontestable is that he has put his money where his mouth is. Courting controversy with every new addition to the oeuvre (and wearily dismissing the charges of violence, racism and general moral pollution – his films are deceptively moral), he has fashioned some of the most significant and unforgettable films of the last twenty-five years.

To quote *Pulp Fiction*, and Travolta's ever-inquisitive hitman Vincent, 'That's a pretty good fucking milkshake.'[2]

Time to get into character…

**Right:** Uma Thurman as Mia Wallace, and her 'five dollar shake'. It was the triumph of *Pulp Fiction* that confirmed Tarantino was no flash in the pan, but a revolutionary who married art and commerce in a way that has remained true for his entire career.

# 'I DIDN'T GO TO FILM SCHOOL, I WENT TO FILMS.'

## Video Archives

Why is Quentin Quentin? The answer is both simple and telling. Late in her pregnancy, Connie Tarantino – henceforth the redoubtable 'Connie' – became hooked on the Western serial 'Gunsmoke', featuring a young Burt Reynolds as Quint Asper, the half-Comanche blacksmith who appeared for three seasons. Connie is half Cherokee, a fact which would contribute an aura of mystery to her extraordinary son. Something she dismissed as 'sensationalism'[1].

'Quint', however, sounded a tad too casual to her ears, and reading William Faulkner's *The Sound and the Fury* led her to the similar but more upstanding 'Quentin', the name belonging to a smart, introspective and somewhat neurotic son of the pivotal Compson clan. So Quentin became Quentin thanks to a mix of high and low culture: the cheesy TV serial paired with a great American novel with its whirling array of charcters and voices. Connie and many of his early friends would know him better as 'Q'.

Connie was only sixteen when Q came kicking and screaming into the world on 27 March 1963 in Knoxville, Tennessee, where he spent the first two years of his life. Exotic tales emerged in the wake of *Reservoir Dogs*' success, describing a hardscrabble infancy with a hillbilly grandfather running a moonshine business. Still in his diapers, he was already on the wrong side of the law. Connie would have to clear that up.

Tarantino has no memory of Knoxville, and never knew his grandparents. That tincture of Huck Finn mentioned in early profiles was a fancy of journalists, although when Dennis Hopper later described him as the 'Mark Twain of the 90s'[2] he wasn't so wide of the mark. They were two great American storytellers with a vivid and sometimes controversial grasp of American idiom.

According to the sardonic Connie, the archetype for tough cookies like Jackie Brown and *Kill Bill*'s Beatrix Kiddo, Tarantino was only born in Tennessee because, for want of a better reason, she decided to go to college in the state where she was born.

**Above:** Burt Reynolds as the half-Comanche Quint Asper posing with the cast of television Western 'Gunsmoke' in 1963. Connie, Tarantino's mother, had been devoted to the series during her pregnancy, which perhaps in turn influenced the baby.

**Opposite:** The television shows Quentin Tarantino avidly watched as a kid laid the foundation for his art. His favourites would continue to be referenced – and offer inspiration – throughout his filmography. The fact that David Carradine starred in 'Kung Fu' influenced his casting in *Kill Bill*, with the show also mentioned directly in *Pulp Fiction*.

**Right:** Burt Reynolds sweet talks Sally Fields in *Smokey and the Bandit II*, a franchise that inspired Tarantino's first attempt at a screenplay at the age of fourteen. Called *Captain Peachfuzz and the Anchovy Bandit*, it featured smart-talking anti-heroes holding up pizza parlours (and remains unmade).

Connie, who had led a peripatetic childhood (native of Tennessee, raised in Ohio, schooled in California), had married not for love but to become an emancipated minor (severing legal ties with her parents). It was, she said, 'a liberated thing'[3]. Tony Tarantino, a part-time actor and law student five years her senior, wasn't around for long. In fact, at the time, he didn't even know his son was born. The marriage was over as soon as she found she was unexpectedly pregnant. 'He told me he couldn't have children,'[4] she smarted.

Finishing college, Connie fled back to the sunshine and freedom of Los Angeles, settling on the ticky-tacky urban sprawl of the South Bay area near the airport, first in El Segundo before finally putting down roots in Torrance. While multicultural, these were affluent middle-class neighbourhoods, something else she wanted to assure prospectors of the Tarantino legend. She soon established a good career for herself in the health-care industry. Bonnie, the homeward bound wife of Tarantino's prickly Jimmie in *Pulp Fiction*, is referred to as a nurse in another *hommage à maman*. In other words, the tenderfoot Tarantino did not go wanting. Nor did he have to tough it out on the streets of South Central.

Connie remained the single dominant presence in Tarantino's upbringing, his moral compass and eternal combatant. She remarried several times to unreliable men. First came local musician Curtis Zastoupil, who adopted the young Quentin. Right into his twenties, Tarantino went by the name Quentin Zastoupil. Connie decided to add the middle name of Jerome, simply because she loved the image of a 'QJZ' mongram. Tarantino once contemplated taking Quentin Jerome as a stage name.

The young Tarantino hung out with his stepfather Curt's coterie of musicians, listening to them banter colourfully about nothing much at all. Even as a toddler, he had picked up on the innate power of profanity. Connie would sigh at the memory of her three-year-old son defiantly retorting *'Bullshit!'* to every request she made of him. She once even resorted to washing his mouth out with soap. The good it did. He just grinned.

He would seldom budge from watching the television set, soaking up movies and shows like 'Kung Fu' (which, of course, featured David Carradine) and 'The Partridge Family'. With a startling facility for recall, he began amassing a treasure trove of pop cultural memories. In *Pulp Fiction* the young Butch Coolidge (Bruce Willis' character) is first seen glued to the screen like a zombie-child watching the creepy 1950s cartoon 'Clutch Cargo' (which the director recalled watching).

Connie would overhear foul-mouthed imprecations echoing through his bedroom door. Bursting in, she would find young Quentin creating scenes with his collection of G.I. Joes, claiming it wasn't his fault that they swore, it was just how his characters spoke. At fourteen he had experimented writing his first screenplay, *Captain Peachfuzz and the Anchovy Bandit*. It was a riff on the Burt Reynolds action-comedy *Smokey and the Bandit*, with car chases, an argot of CB radio terminology, and heroes who held up pizza parlours.

Rather than pay for a babysitter, the liberal-minded Connie took him along to whichever film she was seeing. The American ratings system allowed a child of any age into an R-rated (the nearest equivalent to a UK 18) film as long as an adult accompanied them.

'*Deliverance* scared the living shit out of me,'[5] he recalled, having seen it at the Tarzana 6 in a seminal double with *The Wild Bunch*. He was still only nine years old, and had no idea that Ned Beatty's character was being raped in *Deliverance*'s most shocking moment, but the image was nevertheless filed away in that prodigious memory. Connie's third husband, Jan Bohusch, was the real movie addict. On an average Friday he would take the eager Tarantino to a three, a six, an eight and a midnight movie. Together they saw *Aliens*, *Die Hard*, *The Godfather* films and Brian De Palma movies like *Scarface* and *Body Double*.

**Right:** *Deliverance*, John Boorman's classic and violent tale of city slickers under attack by local woodsmen while on vacation, would stick with an ever-impressionable Quentin Tarantino. Especially so as a liberal-minded Connie took him to see it when he was only nine.

Twelve terrorists. One cop.
The odds are against John McClane…
That's just the way he likes it.

**BRUCE WILLIS**

DIE HARD

TWENTIETH CENTURY FOX Presents A GORDON COMPANY/SILVER PICTURES Production A JOHN McTIERNAN Film BRUCE WILLIS DIE HARD
ALAN RICKMAN ALEXANDER GODUNOV BONNIE BEDELIA Music by MICHAEL KAMEN Visual Effects by RICHARD EDLUND Film Editors FRANK J. URIOSTE, A.C.E.
and JOHN F. LINK Production Designer JACKSON DeGOVIA Director of Photography JAN De BONT Executive Producer CHARLES GORDON Screenplay by JEB STUART and STEVEN E. de SOUZA
Based on the novel by RODERICK THORP Produced by LAWRENCE GORDON and JOEL SILVER Directed by JOHN McTIERNAN Read The Fawcett Paperback
Color by DeLuxe

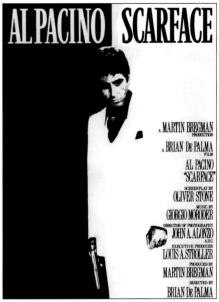

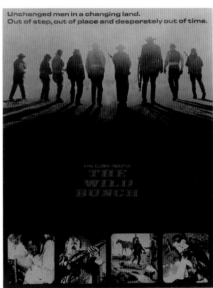

**Above and left:** A trio of impactful film experiences that Tarantino had with Connie's third husband, and movie fan, Jan Bohusch. *Die Hard*, with later *Pulp Fiction* luminary Bruce Willis; *Scarface*, directed by Brian De Palma; and *The Wild Bunch*, whose crumbling machismo can be traced to *Reservoir Dogs*.

Typical of LA's crazy paving of city districts, while Torrance was middle-class, the notoriously ghettoized communities that encircled South Central were only a mile away across the freeway. Tarantino described with relish frequenting the area's 'ghetto theaters.'[6] Each week they would play new kung-fu movies, or a Blaxploitation flick or horror, and he would religiously catch them all. A little further away was an arthouse cinema, where he soaked up French and Italian movies, his tastes broad and eclectic. There beneath the smoky projector beam he first saw the genre-twisting dreams of Jean-Luc Godard, which moved him so very deeply.

Godard's famous aperçu that all you needed to make a film was 'a girl and a gun' was a lesson Tarantino took as gospel, even if the girl would have to wait until his second movie.

He still avidly watched what he called 'the standard Hollywood movies'[7] but his heart was with the contraband delights of *J.D.'s Revenge* and *Lady Kung Fu*. 'You could literally see stuff that you would never see in a Hollywood movie,'[8] he enthused. To his beady eye, the exploitation films were scarcely more lurid than the art films. Sometimes it was hard to tell which one was supposed to be which. It was in that border country that Tarantino would settle as filmmaker.

Later, discussing his approach, he willingly came clean. 'When I started to develop, for lack of a better word my "aesthetic" I loved exploitation movies.'[9] Specifically, it was that jolt of the unexpected. His weren't films designed to comfort; they were meant to rouse us from our slumbers like the electrifying spasm of an adrenalin shot.

It was a lonely vigil. Like Curtis before him, Jan Bohusch would split, leaving Tarantino to his own devices. 'There was nobody in school to talk about movies with,' he bemoaned. 'There was like no adults I could talk with … I had to grow up to meet other adults like myself.'[10]

He would come to make films as a way of having that conversation with the world.

**Right:** Quentin Tarantino was so in awe of French director Jean-Luc Godard, that he and Lawrence Bender named their production company A Band Apart after the French auteur's 1964 classic of a disintegrating criminal gang *Bande à part* (simply meaning a band of outsiders).

His movies talked about other movies, making confidants and geeks of us all.

Tarantino saw hundreds, maybe thousands, of movies from his childhood into his teen years. He was happiest in the dark, learning all he needed to know.

He also read voraciously. Connie pushed the greats on him, but he gravitated to crime fiction. Some would style it pulp fiction. Symbolically, his first brush with the law came when he attempted to steal a copy of Elmore Leonard's *The Switch* from K-Mart. They called the cops, who were only satisfied when Connie grounded the 15-year-old for the whole summer: which meant no movies.

Emerging from house arrest, having ironically caught up on his reading, Tarantino signalled his first urge to act. He asked to join a local community theatre.

There was no doubt that he was a precociously smart kid; his IQ was measured at 160, but school was a prison. He was forever the outsider, dorky-looking and averse to sports. In class, he was disruptive, with a short attention span. He simply couldn't focus. For all their musicality and street smarts, the first drafts of his scripts were a traffic accident of spelling and grammar (QED: *Inglourious Basterds*). He spelled phonetically, and was completely self-taught. 'I was good at reading and I was good at history,' he recalled.[11] History, he said, was like a movie.

So Tarantino regularly played hooky, fuelling the image of him as a street punk drifting at the edge of the law. But he mainly snuck home to watch television, or went off to catch a movie. At sixteen he informed Connie he was dropping out. Connie bravely called his bluff, accepting his decision as long as he got a job. She wanted him to see that life without an education 'wasn't a picnic'.[12]

So began a series of odd jobs, the first of which had a Tarantinoesque ring to it. Still only sixteen, he lied his way into a job at the Pussycat Theater in Torrance – a porn cinema. Connie had no idea, he only told her he was an usher. Tarantino found he had little stomach for what was up on screen, turning his back on images he found too sleazy and an insult to his idea of what movies should be.

**Above:** 1972 Hong Kong action flick *Lady Kung Fu* was typical of the many exploitation films Tarantino took in at nearby 'ghetto theatres'. He was profoundly moved by how you get to see things in them that you would never see in a Hollywood movie.

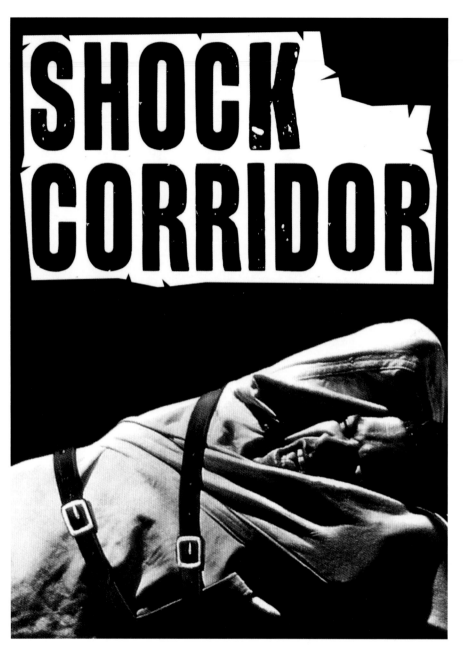

**Above and right:** Quentin Tarantino's first great acting coach James Best, who had starred as the comic sheriff in TV favourite 'The Dukes of Hazzard'. As Tarantino was well aware, Best had also been a favourite of edgy auteur Sam Fuller in films such as *Verboten!* and *Shock Corridor*.

Aside from his failed heist of the K-Mart book department, his other flirtation with the LA underworld amounted to a pile of unpaid parking tickets that landed him in county jail for ten days. His baptism into penal life came as a shock, but he left with a $7,000 backlog in fines cleared and stock of prison lingo to draw on.

A deeper desire was calling. That urge to act rather than act up. In pursuit of his dreams, he moved from community theatre to classes at the James Best Theater Center. Best was celebrated for his role as the inept sheriff Rosco P. Coltrane in the teatime TV hi-jinks of 'The Dukes of Hazzard'. 'He had a class in Toluca Lake, right next to the HoneyBaked Ham,'[13] recalled Tarantino, with a flash of piquant LA detail. He was a big fan. Not necessarily for 'The Dukes of Hazzard', but his earlier work in Samuel Fuller films like *Shock Corridor* and *Verboten!*. Fuller, through his gripping, anti-heroic World War II movies, would have a big influence on *Inglourious Basterds*.

Best was less Method in his approach than methodological, providing sound practical training in how to act for the camera. He helped jobbing actors to pick up five-minute bit parts in TV shows and actually make a living. Advice homaged in *True Romance* (the most nakedly autobiographical of all Tarantino's scripts) where Michael Rapaport's struggling LA actor auditions for real-life TV cop show 'The Return of T.J. Hooker' as a getaway driver.

For one class Tarantino was asked to perform a scene from the 1955 Oscar-winning film *Marty*. Directed by Delbert Mann, Tarantino would emphasize, and written by the revered poet of the streets Paddy Chayefsky. A classmate by the name of Ronnie, who had a paperback of the original play, was impressed, not only with

Tarantino's recall, but the fact he had added an entire monologue about a fountain. 'It's the best thing in there,'[14] he told his friend. It was the first time someone had complimented his writing.

Through Best, he also got a grounding in camera terminology: what was a rack focus or a whip pan. He began to stage and perform long, unbroken monologues he had written, testing them out for the films wandering though his imagination like ghosts. He began thinking more expansively, more like a storyteller.

In any case, his acting career was getting nowhere fast. In fact, prior to *Reservoir Dogs*, his only professional role in ten disheartening years of classes was as an

Elvis impersonator in an episode of the TV sitcom 'The Golden Girls'. With his jutting cartoon-hero jawline and high forehead and a likeable but clumsy bearing, Tarantino was never cut out to be a leading man. He knew that. But he dreamed there were roles out there for him: villains and getaway drivers that might earn him a dollar.

**Above:** Ernest Borgnine and Betsy Blair in 1955 Oscar winner *Marty*. During one acting class, when asked to perform a scene from Paddy Chayefsky's great screenplay from that movie, Tarantino freely added an entire monologue of his own devising.

**Above:** The maestro Leone. If there is one director who has had a greater influence on Tarantino than any other (and Brian De Palma and Jean-Luc Godard come close) then it is the great Italian auteur and his operatic, yet cool, reinvention of the Western.

A sea change was happening. Tarantino was awakening to the idea that he wanted to become a director. He knew so much more about film than his fellow pupils. More to the point, he cared so much more.

'My idols weren't other actors,' he said. 'My idols were directors like Brian De Palma. I decided I didn't want to be in movies. I wanted to make movies.'[15]

Next to De Palma, Tarantino's biggest influences were genre-hopping masters like Howard Hawks and Sergio Leone, the flamboyant maestro of Spaghetti Westerns. His top three films might change depending on his mood, but his founding fathers were carved in stone. On the day he decided to become a director, like a sign from movie heaven, Leone's *Once Upon a Time in the West* was on television. 'It was like a book on how to direct,' marvelled Tarantino, 'a film so well designed. I watched to see how the characters entered the frame and exited the frame.'[16]

**Above:** Jason Robards in Sergio Leone's lavish Spaghetti Western, *Once Upon a Time in the West*. The influence of the 'Spaghettis' can be felt not only in Quentin Tarantino's Westerns, but also in the different genres of *Pulp Fiction* and *Inglourious Basterds*.

**Above:** While Leone's final and most ambitious Spaghetti Western taught Tarantino so much about directing, having given it considered thought, he later determined that *The Good, The Bad and The Ugly* was his favourite film of all time.

Such was Tarantino's obsession with De Palma, the 1970s icon who mixed outrageous, kinetic camera moves with an exploitative, genre-busting kick in films like *Carrie* and the John Travolta thriller *Blow Out* (one of Tarantino's top three), he would keep scrapbooks of all the promotional interviews the director did for his latest film.

On the day of its release, he would ritually go twice: first on his own to the earliest screening, then to the midnight showing with a friend. Video interviews exist of the two directors together – Tarantino melts back into the fan boy while the senior director smiles sheepishly at the adulation.

Tarantino even had the nerve to write to a succession of his favourite directors requesting an interview for a book he was putting together. He wasn't lying exactly; he genuinely intended to write it someday. The likes of Joe Dante and John Milius agreed to meet, and he pressed them for details on how they built a career, thrilled simply to be able to talk movies with real directors.

Meanwhile, Tarantino switched acting classes. Allen Garfield, his new teacher, had worked with Francis Ford Coppola in *The Conversation* and Wim Wenders in *The State of Things*. Moreover, he was located in Beverly Hills. It felt as if he was getting closer to the fountainhead.

During all of this, the dormant acting career, the yearning to direct, and the daily grind of a succession of minimum-wage

jobs, his sanctuary was Video Archives, an eccentric video outlet that occupied a former bicycle shop in a slab-like strip mall on North Sepulveda Boulevard in Manhattan Beach. From 1983 until 1994, when it slipped quietly out of business, the Archives was a daring repository of art films, exploitation flicks and back-catalogue obscurities. It was almost like the shabby, wood-shelved embodiment of Tarantino's cerebral cortex. Here the French New Wave prevailed over Schwarzenegger.

In retrospect, as the Tarantino story has been told and retold in restaurants and bars and boardrooms, it became the hippest video joint in America. In truth, it barely broke even, but for Tarantino it was as close to heaven as you could find in the South Bay.

The personnel would ebb and flow, hired, fired and rehired as they fell in and out of favour with the generally absentee

manager Lance Lawson. On $4 an hour, the likes of Rand Vossler, Jerry Martinez, Stevo Polyi and Rowland Wafford could be found slouched behind the counter. Then there was Roger Avary, the hippyish art-school dropout with Tom Petty-like tresses who had got as far as messing around with Super-8 cameras, stop-motion and writing scripts. But the loudest know-all with the biggest brain, the unkempt sun around which they all orbited, was Tarantino. He had wandered in one day and got into an argument over De Palma with Lance, and was still fuming four hours later. The next day he returned to debate Leone. So effusive was he about movies, and so good at dissuading a customer from renting *Top Gun* and instead risking their night's entertainment on a Godard classic, that Lance had no option but to offer him a job.

**Above:** Mickey (Woody Harrelson) and Mallory (Juliette Lewis) in Oliver Stone's *Natural Born Killers*. Quentin Tarantino's original screenplay for 'NBK' was one of the first things he wrote, and actually was conceived as a screenplay that Clarence was writing within the screenplay for *True Romance*.

The Video Archivists would control what played on the screens, running their own film festivals in miniature, a cultural nexus of squalling debate. It was here that Tarantino furthered his film education, a kid loose in a candy store.

'We were the video store generation, right after the film-school generation,' said Avary, Tarantino's chief rival and soon enough closest friend, 'the first generation of people who wanted to be filmmakers who had grown up alongside computers, videos and the information highway.'[17]

Video changed everything. Before the advent of the plastic film cassette, the great catalogue of cinematic achievement was

# 'The Video Archivists were all working on scripts... Tarantino was the only one with the drive to transform one of his scripts into a film.'

unreachable. Once a film had passed out of the cinemas, you were a slave to the lucky dip of television. Renting 16mm prints was for rich hobbyists. With video suddenly you could get your hands on something like 20,000 titles. According to film historian Peter Biskind, video heralded a new generation of director able to circumvent

film school and wilfully ignore the holy writ of the 'great tradition'[18] curated by academics that had fashioned the thinking of the movie brat generation of Scorsese and Spielberg. The video store geeks responded with equal fervour to martial arts movies and Renoir. The 'civilising influences'[19] of film culture went unheeded and, 'a new brutalism'[20] was born.

The Video Archivists were all working on scripts, staking out a future that for most of them would never come. But it was Tarantino who channelled their crackpot debates and comic routines into his side projects, his ear already attuned to the music of idle banter. Tarantino was also the only one with the drive to transform one of his scripts into a film. *My Best Friend's Birthday*, or at least what remains of it, was made for little more than $5,000 via credit cards, loans and whatever he could spare from Video Archives wages. It was made in collaboration with a screenwriter he had met at the James Best Theater Center named Craig Hamann.

With similar dreams of making it as an actor, they quickly hit it off. Both possessed an encyclopaedic knowledge of movies and what they considered a healthy disregard for the way things were supposed to be done. Together they wrote a buddy comedy in the style of 1950s stars Dean Martin and Jerry Lewis (Tarantino was going through a screwball comedy phase). It was essentially a rewrite of a short autobiographical script Hamann had written in 1984 about the attempts of a well-meaning buddy to provide his best friend with a birthday to remember only for his plans to go hilariously awry.

The credits go like this: Tarantino was director, producer and editor, Hamann was producer, Rand Vossler the sometime cinematographer and Avary a bit of everything else. Tarantino and Hamann starred as Clarence (the unfortunate friend) and Mickey (the birthday boy). One of the first things Clarence does for his friend is hire him a prostitute, giving her a key to his house. Close observers will spot the fingerprints of *True Romance*.

Using affordable black and white stock, *My Best Friend's Birthday* was largely filmed at the Tarantino home. The eternally understanding Connie had to move out for three months. Following three years of, as Tarantino put it, 'just shooting off and on'[21] they finally raised the money to take the film to the lab. Tarantino was heartbroken. What he saw on screen was far from what he had imagined in his head; it was unfunny, amateur-looking, and there were plot holes the size of Nevada. When a couple of uninsured cans of film were ruined in a lab accident, rather than fight a losing battle Tarantino left it unfinished. There were few regrets. 'I didn't know what I was doing,'[22] he reflected philosophically. Still, what better experience than failing to make a film?

He now had a sense of what to do, and, better still, what not to do. He began feverishly writing, although his friendship with Hamann never recovered. The separation was only briefly interrupted when Tarantino called him onto the set of *Pulp Fiction* to educate Uma Thurman and John Travolta on what it was like to OD on heroin.

The source of Tarantino's burst of creativity was Avary. He had mentioned something he had been writing. There wasn't much to it yet, it was little more than a short about a couple on the run called *The Open Road*, so when Tarantino asked if he could rewrite it, Avary accepted. 'Months went by,' he recalled, 'and then Quentin returned with this stack of papers, handwritten – nearly illegible, words phonetically spelled.'[23]

This astonishing 500-page outpouring (Avary may be the only other person to have read it in its entirety) was the primordial soup of Tarantino's fictional universe: an LA underworld of grifters and hitmen, hookers and thieves, littered with references to other movies, TV shows, crime fiction and quirks

of pop culture. It contained *True Romance* and *Natural Born Killers* in their entirety, and slivers of what would become *Pulp Fiction*. Here too, Avary noticed, was the Video Archive jive lifted from the shop floor.

'It barely contained any of my original screenplay,' he laughed, 'but he had brought an emotional soul to it beyond what I had written.'[24]

At Avary's insistence, he began to break it down into workable, typed-up screenplays. First to emerge was *True Romance*. Then came *Natural Born Killers*. Then after setting aside what would be *Pulp Fiction*, he started to enlarge on his idea about a gang of jewel thieves gathering after a heist goes wrong.

While legend has Tarantino plucked straight into stardom from behind the

**Above:** John Travolta styles it out in *Pulp Fiction*, another screenplay whose roots stretch right back to Quentin Tarantino's first serious attempts at writing during his Video Archive days.

counter of Video Archives, he had long since departed the rental outlet when he started on *Reservoir Dogs* in 1989. There was every danger he might dream his life away in the cocoon of the video store. He had to get practical about being a filmmaker, but the rent still had to be paid. For a time he sold bottom-rung video titles for low-level film distribution outlet Imperial, using his knack for improvisation to call up stores and claim to be, say, a housewife from Dubuque in search of a particular Imperial title.

Through its production arm, Imperial enabled him to enlarge his circle of contacts, and he began to scratch out a living as a professional screenwriter, eventually sacrificing his desire to direct *True Romance* when he was offered the minimum Writer's Guild fee of $30,000 for it. He was commissioned to do uncredited rewrites on *Past Midnight* (a tawdry Rutger Hauer thriller about a sexy ex-con for Tarantino-completests alone) before being hired by the KNB EFX Group, an effects house specializing in horror-movie make-up, to come up with a script for an infomercial-cum-movie entitled *From Dusk Till Dawn*. Scripts were now circling like jets waiting to land at LAX, and Tarantino formed a partnership with Video Archives buddy

Rand Vossler in a doomed attempt to make *Natural Born Killers*.

Still, Tarantino liked to joke ruefully that if you had wanted to contact him, you simply address a letter to Quentin Tarantino, Outskirts of the Film Industry, Los Angeles! But he knew *Reservoir Dogs* was special. If he could get it into the right hands, things could finally happen for him.

And if fate wasn't going to cut him any slack, he could just about make it for the $30,000 fee from *True Romance* – money no-one could tell him what to do with. It might only play at obscure film festivals, but it would put him on the map as a director.

'I knew I was going to shoot a film. I *knew* it. This was the one. This was *achievable.*'[25]

**Abovet:** The mammoth Mexican stand-off in Tony Scott's adaptation of *True Romance*. Effectively, *True Romance* was Tarantino's very first screenplay from this era, which he had fully intended to be his first film. It is also his most autobiographical work – if you discount the Mexican stand-offs.

# 'I MADE THIS MOVIE FOR MYSELF, AND EVERYONE IS INVITED.' [24]

## Reservoir Dogs

The phenomenon of Quentin Tarantino began for real with a chance encounter at a party. The frustrated director-in-waiting found himself talking to a charismatic young tyro producer from the Bronx named Lawrence Bender. Bender was another failed actor, but he had at least graced the New York stage – including in a production of *A Midsummer Night's Dream* with Christopher Walken – and flirted with professional dancing.

With a dancer's slender frame and thoughtful, elfin features, he was the yin to Tarantino's yang. Whereas his future business partner could be excitable and scatterbrained, Bender possessed East Coast guile and a flare for organization.

Relocation to Los Angeles to further his acting career proved fruitless, so he switched to producing films. Out of nothing, he managed to get two films off the ground, the better of which was a slasher pic called *Intruder* (in which a maniac stalks an all-night supermarket) directed by a mutual filmmaking friend in Scott Spiegel. For the record, the other was a misbegotten family drama based on Charlie Sheen's poetry called *Tale of Two Sisters*.

It was at Spiegel's party that Bender and Tarantino ran into one another. Tarantino had got to know Spiegel in his Imperial

Entertainment days. Plus he was a huge fan of *Intruder*, having seen it four times. Bender realized that they had actually met once before, appropriately enough standing in line for a movie (a late night 3D double-bill). Bender also recalled that he'd read a 'really cool'[1] script called *True Romance*, but the chances were it was by another Tarantino.

'That's my script!'[2] the one and only Tarantino burst out, grinning like a clown.

At Spiegel's suggestion, Bender came to read the original screenplay for *Natural Born Killers*, which had been wilting on the vine for two years. He didn't really connect with where Tarantino was taking it (daringly Bender recommended a rewrite), suspecting the director-in-waiting had reached his 'shelf-life' on his killing-spree romance. Then Tarantino mentioned another script that he was working on called *Reservoir Dogs*.

**Above:** Quentin Tarantino at 28, delivering the opening lines of his first feature film as the doomed Mr. Brown. The pre-credits breakfast scene was designed to show that despite being crooks, these guys were people, talking like it's a normal day. None of them knows that they might just be a

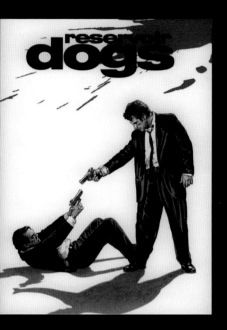

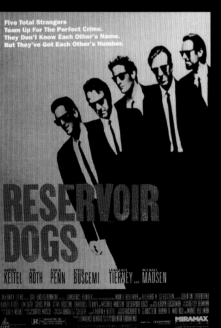

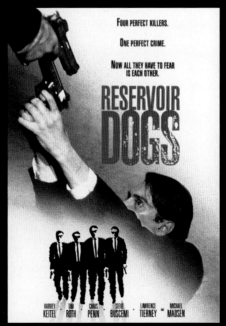

**Above and left:** The famous imagery of black suits and shades, which dominated the poster campaigns, was drawn from movie mythology rather than life. To Tarantino the idea was that any witnesses would describe them as all looking the same, but real-life career criminal Eddie Bunker (Mr. Blue) laughed away the suggestion that thieves would ever dress for the occasion.

'It's a low budget movie,' he promised, 'because it all takes place in one garage where all these guys who pull a heist come back to, and you know something has gone badly wrong. But you never see the heist.'[3]

That was key – the whole film was all about the *aftermath*.

During the writing, Tarantino had jettisoned an idea of providing tiny, almost subliminal, glimpses of the calamitous heist like flashes of gunfire. While in rehearsal he had encouraged the actors to plot out the heist, mapping out the jewellery store in chalk, in order to create a sense memory of what had gone down.

Impressed with the work in progress, Bender suggested this was their project. He asked for a year to find backing, but Tarantino was in no mood to wait. After years of false dawns and empty promises, he itched to take his destiny back into his own hands. He offered Bender a two-month

option on *Reservoir Dogs*. By which time if he hadn't landed a deal, Tarantino would go ahead and make it himself. He would play Mr. Pink (the chatterbox, tip-averse 'professional' eventually taken by Steve Buscemi) and Bender would be Nice Guy Eddie (the mobile-phone wielding hothead whose garish shell-suit was filled by Chris Penn). They would find a garage or warehouse, complete the cast with the Video Archive crew and hungry actors he knew from class, and make it for next to nothing.

There were no lawyers involved. Bender simply scribbled the agreement down on a scrap of paper and they both signed it, forging a partnership that lasted for over twenty years.

The finished screenplay repaid Bender's faith in full. It was extraordinary: complex yet funny, violent and tragic, a genre piece with dialogue worthy of Eugene O'Neill, if

the eminent playwright had been fluent with the guttersnipe patois of the South Bay. Two months was a blink of an eye by the geological pace of Hollywood decision-making, but displaying some Brooklyn grit Bender went to work. Real progress soon came when Monte Hellman, the cult director of *Two Lane Blacktop*, read the script. Fascinated by the sudden shifts from comedy to brutality, he was keen to direct.

Meeting Hellman for lunch at a Hollywood hamburger joint, Tarantino's heart sank. Naturally, he was a huge fan of Hellman's work, but this was his baby and he couldn't give it up. Seeing the passion bottled up in this guy, Hellman willingly came on as a producer to help him get it made. He even offered to mortgage his home and a tract of Texan real estate to raise a few hundred thousand dollars.

Then fortune did its bit for the cause.

**Opposite:** Partners in crime – director Quentin Tarantino and producer Lawrence Bender had gelled straightaway, signing their pact to somehow get *Reservoir Dogs* to the big screen on a scrap of paper and forming a working partnership that lasted for twenty years.

**Above:** Actor James Taylor and director Monte Hellman on the set of Hellman's drag racing cult classic *Two-Lane Blacktop*. Through Bender, Hellman was one of the first to read *Reservoir Dogs*, and was so taken with the mix of humour and violence in the script that he offered to mortgage his house to help get it made.

**Right:** Naturally, Hellman was a hero of Tarantino's. Even so, when Hellman hinted that he wanted to direct *Reservoir Dogs*, the young writer was happy to set him straight. He was going to direct it himself and that's all there was to it. Hellman was so taken with Tarantino's passion, he remained as executive producer.

'If we could have anyone in the world,' Bender mused, 'Harvey Keitel would be the guy.'

– Lawrence Bender

**Left:** The great Harvey Keitel in 1990 noir thriller *The Two Jakes*. Keitel's miraculous involvement would literally be the making of *Reservoir Dogs*. He had at first contemplated playing Mr. Pink or Mr. Blonde (there was no mention of specific ages in the script), but soon realized he was the ideal Mr. White.

**Opposite:** A young Keitel with Robert De Niro in Martin Scorsese's 1976 classic *Taxi Driver*. Keitel sensed there was a common denominator between the young Scorsese and this new kid: a certain intensity, a certain vulnerability, a certain insight.

Bender hadn't entirely relinquished his acting ambitions, and one day after class he and his acting coach Peter Floor got talking about the heist thriller he was trying to get off the ground. Floor asked whom in a perfect world he imagined as the lead.

'If we could have anyone in the world,' Bender mused, 'Harvey Keitel would be the guy.'

Floor looked him in the eye and a miracle began to unfold. 'Well, my wife Lily knows him from the Actors' Studio. Let me give it to her and if she likes it, maybe she can give it to him.'

Lily Parker, Floor's wife, loved what she read, and passed it on to Keitel, an acquaintance at the famous New York acting school. Bender returned home one Sunday afternoon to hear a familiar voice on his answerphone: 'This is Harvey Keitel speaking. I read the script *Reservoir Dogs*, and I'd like to talk to you about it.'[4]

Destiny had called. But Tarantino's gifts were forging their own luck. No-one, anywhere, was writing like this. Keitel thought it one of the most provocative scripts he had read in years. He related to how it played on ideas of camaraderie and redemption. It shared the intensity he found in Scorsese's early material. Keitel too offered his help to get it made.

Tarantino was in clover. Like Bender, Keitel was just about his favourite actor. 'I was fifteen years old when I saw him in *Taxi Driver* and *The Duellists*.'[5] Naturally, he'd since seen everything he'd done.

Keitel's commitment made the project vastly more attractive to Live Entertainment. Although Richard Gladstein, their likeable vice president of production, claimed he would still have made the film (if on a smaller budget). Unless, that is, Tarantino turned out to be 'a complete idiot'[6]. Live had established itself in the video industry ploughing a horror furrow, including *Silent Night, Deadly Night 3: Better Watch Out*, directed by Hellman. Gladstein was sent hundreds of scripts every month, but Hellman was canny enough to drop Tarantino's script off at his home address. Flicking to the opening page as he made his way back from his mailbox, it read, '*Reservoir Dogs*, Written and Directed by Quentin Tarantino'[7]. Then below that: 'Final Draft'. Some chutzpah, he thought, for an unknown.

Gladstein soon discovered why. He downed *Reservoir Dogs* in one glorious gulp, unable to stop. 'I was just blown away,'[8] he said. Within Tarantino's fevered thriller, a gang of professional crooks – he was insistent they were not gangsters – are hired to pull off a diamond heist in an unspecified LA jewellery store. To keep the operation secure, they are all strangers to one another. In a splendidly comic scene, each receives a colour-related codename – Mr. White, Mr. Brown, Mr. Pink etc – and they squabble over the coolest designations. 'Be thankful you're not Mr. Yellow,'[9] snaps Joe Cabot, the bristling mobster in charge, to an indignant Mr. Pink.

Such was the character-driven nature of the film, Tarantino could have cast it sixteen different ways and had sixteen different movies. But its dramatic urgency depended on finding the right chemistry for this ill-met gang of hoods and their 'tough guy existentialism'[10].

'We wanted the right balance,' he insisted. 'Everyone had to be different, different rhythms, different looks, different personalities, different acting styles.'[11]

Having the perfect Mr. White in place, and Keitel made it clear that was where he was leaning, allowed Tarantino to assemble the film around his benefactor. After a series of LA auditions at Keitel's Malibu beach house, which landed them Michael Madsen (whom they had courted by sneaking in the script with his usual courier) as the closet psycho Mr. Blonde, Keitel suggested Tarantino and Bender come out to New

York and get a taste of the more acerbic East Coast actors. He was even willing to cover their airfares and hotel bills. While taking a drink at Manhattan's famous Russian Tea Rooms, the moment had come to offer Keitel a co-producing credit. 'I've been waiting for you to ask,'[12] he replied.

*Reservoir Dogs* revealed a gift for casting that has never let Tarantino down. He knew these characters by heart; they were his creations, extensions of himself, so he could sense instinctively when they stepped through the door.

New York yielded Steve Buscemi as a knockout Mr. Pink, and an early meeting with Samuel L. Jackson for Mr. Orange. Jackson wasn't his Orange, but a seed was planted.

Tarantino met the British actor Tim Roth in LA on the Fox lot, where they had set up their next set of casting sessions. He asked which character Roth wanted to play, Blonde

or Pink? 'Orange,'[13] he replied. Tarantino hadn't seen that coming. Orange, fittingly maybe, was the hardest Dog to picture.

Roth liked the complexity of the part. How he was 'a fiction within the fiction.'[14] In a twist that sends our whole perception of the film spinning in another direction, Orange emerges as the quasi-protagonist: an undercover cop named Freddy Newandyke, the rat in the nest, given a chapter of backstory where he is shown learning his part, rehearsing the kind of anecdote that makes him sound authentically like a crook.

**Below:** On set, Tim Roth gets into the backstory of undercover cop Freddy Newandyke (aka Mr. Orange) with Tarantino. Notice the first sighting of two typical Tarantino motifs: Freddy's Speed Racer T-shirt and a discontinued brand of 1970s breakfast cereal.

Like all of the Dogs, he is putting on a performance: learning his lines, auditioning, ready to play a part. It's a meta-fictional routine repeated in *Pulp Fiction*, when Jules and Vincent pause before crashing in on their quarry in order to get into character.

'That's a motif that runs through all these gangster guys,'[15] explained Tarantino. They are like a cross between criminals and actors and children parroting the routines they see on TV.

The remainder of the gang was filled out with crime author and former con (a bona fide Dog) Eddie Bunker, Chris Penn (Sean Penn's young brother), the 1950s character actor Lawrence Tierney (who was inclined to grouch) and Tarantino himself. Hadn't he become a director to help the out-of-work actor inside? He saved Mr. Brown for himself, lifting a choice slice of Mr. Pink's dialogue for his own grand entrance – the opening lines

of the film, pontificating on the meaning behind Madonna's 'Like A Virgin', as the Video Archive boys used to do.

And what of the name? Was there a meaning behind '*Reservoir Dogs*'? The title had actually come before the movie. It sounded like a movie he would want to see; all he needed to do was find the right story to go with it. As for an actual meaning … Well, it definitely meant something to Tarantino, but he didn't like to say. After the film became a hit, he was 'knocked out'[16] by the number of people telling him what they thought it might allude to. The minute he explained himself, all that speculation would stop.

There were, of course, meetings with moneymen and marketeers, the uncool citizens of the Hollywood drag, where the obscure title was questioned. How about *The Big Shootout?*

He laughed. 'I didn't want any of that, so I told them, "It's an expression used in French New Wave gangster films meaning 'rat'. It's in *Breathless*, it is in *Bande à part*." A total lie, but they believed it. They hadn't seen those movies.'[17]

Connie claimed a more mundane origin for the title. Namely, her son's appalling French pronunciation. Back at the Video Archives, recommending Louis Malle's *Au revoir les enfants* it always came out as 'Reservoir Dogs'.

**Above:** The imperious Dogs pose for the camera at Johnnie's Coffee Shop on Wilshire Boulevard. From the left: Mr. White (Harvey Keitel), Mr. Orange (Tim Roth), Mr. Brown (Quentin Tarantino), Mr. Pink (Steve Buscemi), Mr. Blue (Eddie Bunker), Joe Cabot (Lawrence Tierney), Mr. Blonde (Michael Madsen), and Nice Guy Eddie (Chris Penn).

**Above:** After years of striving, Quentin Tarantino finally gets to directs his first movie, somehow entirely on his own terms. The cast and crew would shoot for five weeks in rundown quarters of Los Angeles and a mortuary in Highland Park that was later destroyed in the 1994 LA earthquake.

Barely weeks from shooting, Tarantino landed one of the prestigious slots at the Sundance Institute (six filmmakers were taken out of thousands of applications) in Utah. Designed as a two-week instructive lab for prospective filmmakers, they could shoot putative scenes and receive feedback from panels of established filmmakers. Tarantino did test runs of various sequences from *Reservoir Dogs* in long unbroken takes, his off-kilter, prolix style coming naturally. His first panel depressed him by demanding he cut into his scenes. But the second panel, featuring Terry Gilliam, got excited. 'Believe in yourself,'[18] commanded Gilliam. Coupled with that electric dialogue, they sensed this was something different.

*Reservoir Dogs* filmed over the sweltering summer of 1991 – there are behind-the-scenes shots of Tierney and Penn going shirtless before the camera rolled to save on the sweat – in ratty, 1970s-looking LA locations. The rendezvous was in fact a mortuary in Highland Park (sadly demolished after the LA earthquake of 1994). There are coffins under wraps, and the car on which we find Mr. Blonde perched in a lovely theatrical reveal is a hearse. The very first scene they shot was of Madsen's Vic Vega (aka Mr. Blonde) arriving in Joe's office, where he and Nice Guy Eddie – old buddies – begin to wrestle like kids. Bender was wise to the fact they should kick off with something simple. Start conservative, enrol the backers in your

process, and they're not going to worry about you. Even as he began to elaborate with low angles, doorways, mirrors and 360-degree circling shots, contrasting the heated theatricality of the warehouse with the jagged dynamism on the streets, Tarantino genuinely feared he could get fired.

Five weeks later, he wrapped his first movie and the world was a different place.

With Live Entertainment only providing video distribution, the Sundance Film Festival was their best chance to land a theatrical release. Independent distributors descended on the snow-cloaked Park City every January to fill their arthouse schedules and, hopefully, snare among them that title with the right DNA to stir the mainstream.

This often led to feeding frenzies, in which the New York-based Miramax was the biggest shark in the pool. It had made hay with Steven Soderbergh's intriguing Sundance hit *sex, lies and videotape* and cannily marketed *The Crying Game* to enormous success on the shock value of its gender-bending twist.

Harvey Weinstein, the louder and meaner of the two brothers that ran the company, already well known for his bullying business tactics, would be another godfather to Tarantino's career before a well-documented fall from grace.

Let loose at his very first film festival, it was as if Tarantino had been given a free pass to Disneyland. He was watching films, and talking to everyone, holding forth with

best Video Archive jives. And everyone was talking about this grinning galoot and his wild movie. Once his film screened, *Reservoir Dogs* was *all* anyone was taking about. The prissy old-Sundance values were being worked over by his film's spiky machismo, street snarl and the ear-slitting scene had sparked a rash of walkouts.

**Above:** After years too of striving to be an actor, Tarantino wasn't going to forgo the opportunity of casting himself. Although, his heart was set on playing Mr. Pink, his head told him the large role would tax his multi-tasking skills, so he stuck with doomed Mr. Brown.

What was really shocking the Sundance crowd, however, was that *Reservoir Dogs* was thrilling. The fizzing, discursive dialogue; the supple twisting of genre conventions; the caustic yet vulnerable performances; the tingling mix of the very real and the brazenly self-conscious – the sleepy, snowbound town had seen nothing like it. It might have rankled that the in-crowd closed ranks and awarded best film of 1992 to Alexandre Rockwell's *In the Soup*, but it was *Reservoir Dogs* that the distributors were chasing most eagerly, and Miramax swiftly mobilized to snap up the film.

The critics were already onboard. If there were those who questioned the lack of a moral centre, Tarantino was cheered along by heavyweights like Vincent Canby in *The New York Times*: 'Mr. Tarantino has a fervid imagination, but he also has the strength and talent to control it.' He was seen as herald of a new wave of Hollywood filmmaker, culturally aware, proudly reckless, and fired up. *Reservoir Dogs*, said Kenneth Turan in the *Los Angeles Times*, 'is as much a calling card as a movie, an audacious high-wire act announcing that he is here and to be reckoned with.'

It appeared as if Tarantino had arrived fully formed. It wasn't simply character and dialogue – here was a virtuoso of structure. *Reservoir Dogs* essentially plays across about one hour of real time (the period spent in the warehouse as the survivors wrestle with what happened, what to do next and generally disintegrate), supplemented by backstory covering Newandyke's training

to go undercover; Vic Vega, fresh out of the clink; and the introduction of the crew at their garrulous pre-credits breakfast. Movie time is mixed with real time: genre characters, slick-looking crooks, filling in the gaps with lifelike chatter.

Tarantino was firm that these episodes preceding the main action are not flashbacks. He thought of the disparate parts of the film as chapters in a novel, each with a different perspective. 'What I am doing as narrator is rearranging the order in the way I want you to get the information. The chapters don't necessarily run consecutively.'[19]

Rearranging time also allowed him to mess with his audience. How we are lulled by all that growling amongst the Dogs about Madonna and the ethics of tipping, only to be jarred awake by Roth's agonised squeals, and the sight of him, leaking blood like a stuck pig on the backseat of a getaway car. The effect is utterly disorientating. As if we've blacked out and suddenly come round.

The script doesn't flinch from racial epithets, homophobic slurs, sexism, and a steady patina of expletives, but it makes music from them. Tarantino was well aware he was opening himself up for criticism in an era grown lily-livered with political correctness. In interview after interview, he insisted that he was letting the characters be who they are. Fractured tough guys shielded in Ray Bans with their compendiums of LA street slang spliced into pop cultural sermons archived in his voluminous memory. He was a Method writer: all their voices flowed out of him like a river.

**Right:** The immortal sight of the Reservoir Dogs going to work along Eagle Rock Boulevard to the groove of the George Baker Selection's 'Little Green Bag' came to define not only Quentin Tarantino's career but an entire era.

He thrilled to the effect his characters were having on audiences and critics. He intended to shatter the 'square dance'[20] mentality of Hollywood filmmaking. And the ear-slicing centrepiece, which garnered such notoriety, was the ultimate proof he could have the audience dancing to his fiddle. Drown the film in blood and the audience becomes anaesthetized. The nerve-jangling thrill of Tarantino is in anticipation of violence – in imagining what lies ahead.

Indeed, Tarantino actually turns the camera away at the crucial moment. There had been a take that drank in the ear slicing in all its graphic detail, but the scene is so tautly choreographed it doesn't need it. The sound of Stealers Wheel's languorously catchy 'Stuck in the Middle with You' on the radio (that whimsical extra character), the icy-calm invocation of psychosis in Madsen's dance, his almost intimate expression (it's a great performance), and finding the cold blade in his boot delaying the visceral moment.

To get into the mind-set for the five-hours it would take to shoot the scene, Madsen had talked Kirk Baltz, who plays the hostage cop Marvin Nash, to get into the boot of his car while he drove him around

the block to establish the victim-perpetrator dynamic. Baltz may have regretted agreeing, for Madsen ended up touring around town for forty-five minutes, stopping at a Taco Bell to grab a Coke (inspiring the improv of him nonchalantly sipping on a soda) before returning to a bemused production, and letting his bruised co-star out of the trunk. Tarantino loved it.

The walkouts came because people couldn't bear the anticipation. Those who stuck it out didn't know whether to shriek or laugh. Exactly as Tarantino had designed it, foot-tapping to the beat we become complicit in the violence.

'I sucker punched you,' he delighted. 'You're supposed to laugh until I stop you laughing.'[21]

This isn't violence per se; this is style. Early in Tarantino's autodidactic film education, he had loved the *Abbott and Costello* comedies from the 1940s where they meet Frankenstein or the Mummy. 'The genius of the concept of a horror film and a comedy together – two great tastes that taste great together.'[22]

It sounded like an advert for the concession counter.

Nevertheless, he spent many months in the wake of *Reservoir Dogs'* success fending off accusations of making violence look dangerously attractive. Don't lay the whole moral quandary at my door, he blasted back. As he saw it, violence on screen was a very cinematic thing, something detached from life. These were his musical numbers.

'What I find offensive is that Merchant-Ivory shit,' he hollered to an ecstatic crowd at a post-screening Q&A in Sundance. 'Violence is one of the greatest things you can do in cinema …'[23] Place handcuffs on an artist and you stifle art.

To criticize his film as brutal only for its own sake is to neglect the slow, sticky, realistic death of Mr. Orange, belly-shot and bleeding fatally throughout the real-time of the film. Each day the unit had to peel Roth from the floor, clean up the mess, and then repour his pooling blood the next morning. Roth's screeching, desperate cries punch through the film's cool veneer, and form the focal point for Mr. White's emotional crisis.

All the profane verbal arias, the consciously cool imagery and bang-bang excitement enclose powerful themes of loyalty and betrayal between friends. No good deed goes unpunished in the crooked criminal world Tarantino was forging, and these would become the unifying themes of his career. Decode his fiction and you'll soon locate the indifferent biological father, the inconstant stepfathers and the lonely only child finding solace in movies.

'I made this movie for myself,' he said, 'and everyone is invited.'[24]

**Above:** Hostage cop Marvin Nash (Kirk Baltz) bears witness to the Dogs' disintegrating group dynamic. While Tarantino was determined that the audience should remain unaware of exactly what happened in the sabotaged heist, during rehearsal the actors had staged the robbery to give them a sense memory of what had gone down.

**Right:** Mr. White (Harvey Keitel) tends to Mr. Orange (Tim Roth), who is realistically bleeding to death over the hour of real-time portrayed in the film. Roth had to be be stuck back down to the bloodstained floor every morning, and the gory puddle cleaned up at the end of the day.

It was clear Tarantino would only ever make films on his own terms. Miramax had remonstrated with him that if he removed the ear slicing, they would have a mainstream hit on their hands. But if he didn't hold firm, he would never regain control of his material again. That scene set the seal on who he was to be as a filmmaker. 'That moment,' he recognized, 'decided my career for all time.'[25]

After further film festival screenings in Cannes and Toronto, *Reservoir Dogs* opened to satisfactory rather than spectacular business in the USA. Released on 23 October 1992, it did well enough to earn its money back, but no more, making $2,832,029. It was Tarantino who broke out. He charmed the press with his motorboat repartee, brazen honesty and quaint cartoon expressions, everything he approved of falling under the catchall definition 'cool'. If especially noteworthy it was 'fucking cool'.

Following the American launch, Tarantino took himself on a world tour, first to festivals all over Europe, then further afield to Asia. He was tireless, unable to stop, thrilling at the chance to see the world and talk about movies with no-one to silence him. His celebrity soared. And if he was running the risk of overexposure, the cult growing around his personality was having a beneficial effect.

Away from America, *Reservoir Dogs* became a smash hit. In France, this *enfant terrible*'s great debut would run for an entire year. In the UK, the film's reception encompassed the full gamut of the Tarantino effect. Conflated with the video nasty controversy (in which the media became excited about certain violent titles inspiring copycat crimes), it ended up being banned on video, along with another Harvey Keitel episode of tough guy existentialism, *Bad Lieutenant*. Tarantino was thrilled. 'The easiest way to kill the excitement and cult of something is to make it accessible.'[26] The film played for months making $6 million, double the American box office.

By Tarantino's return, America was stirring and the phone was ringing off the hook at Video Archives with would-be filmmakers offering their services. Tarantino was the rock star alternative to the bubblegum mainstream, and *Reservoir Dogs* sold an unprecedented 900,000 video copies, three times the expected number.

In another minor hullabaloo in the film's wake, the UK movie magazine *Empire* cottoned on to similarities between *Reservoir Dogs* and Ringo Lam's Hong

Kong hit *City on Fire*, which featured a cop going undercover at a jewel heist (you could equally cite Stanley Kubrick's racetrack noir *The Killing*, with its fragmenting gang). Was he guilty of plagiarism? Tarantino's response was to have a T-shirt made of the article. As he told them, completely unabashed, 'I steal from every single movie ever made.'[27]

**Above:** Mr. Pink (Steve Buscemi) and Mr. White (Keitel) in the first of the film's Mexican stand-offs. While the film did respectable business at the American box office, it took off in Europe, where the cult of Quentin Tarantino was launched.

# 'I THINK OF THEM AS LIKE OLD GIRLFRIENDS...'

## True Romance, Natural Born Killers and From Dusk Till Dawn

In the wake of *Reservoir Dogs*, three further Quentin Tarantino scripts went into production with unprecedented haste. Each was written long before *Reservoir Dogs* started barking. Each began life with the manageable ambitions of a first film. Together they are an object lesson in the seismic impact he would have on Hollywood in the early 1990s.

There was only one director who could truly do justice to a Tarantino script. And that was Quentin Tarantino. Sometimes the only thing worse than being ignored by Hollywood is *not* being ignored by Hollywood.

*True Romance*, of course, was the first script to be extracted from Tarantino's protean crime-epic *The Open Road* in 1987. Unsurprisingly, it is his most autobiographical story. Clarence (the name spilling over from *My Best Friend's Birthday*) is a clear alter ego: pining for love, ritually taking in a Sonny Chiba double-bill on his birthday (then going for pie), and working at a Detroit comic-book (instead of a Los Angeles video) store, where his boss goes by the name of Lance. He readily admitted, 'It's one hundred percent my consciousness.'[1] Events depart for more imaginative realms when Clarence falls for

a hooker named Alabama, and guided by his spirit-guide Elvis shoots her pimp (echoing *Taxi Driver*). The couple then hotfoot it for LA to offload a stash of mob cocaine to a garrulous movie producer.

It began more complex than the linear film that resulted, with, he explained, more of an 'answers first, questions later'[2] structure like *Reservoir Dogs*. In only the second scene, we meet white-Rasta pimp Drexl and his business associate Floyd holding forth on why he 'don't be eatin' pussy'[3] (a scene heavily trimmed in fear of a ratings disaster). Back then there were strictly no takers. Not for the script, and certainly not for the script with Tarantino as director, and the rejection letters could be severe. 'How dare you send me this fucking piece of shit,' railed one response, 'are you out of your fucking mind?'[4]

**Above:** While often dubbed an overnight success, Quentin Tarantino had been writing professionally for years, and even before the release of *Reservoir Dogs*, the scripts for *True Romance* and *Natural Born Killers* were in circulation.

**Right:** Patricia Arquette as retired hooker and dream girl Alabama Whitman in *True Romance*. Tarantino chose the name Alabama in homage to a character Pam Grier plays in the grindhouse flick *Women in Cages*. There was originally a line in the script where Clarence actually points this out.

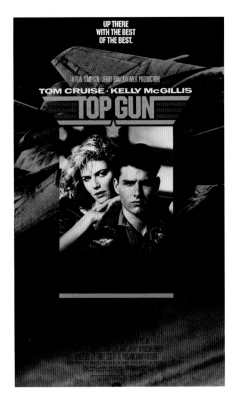

**Above left:** Back in his Video Archives days, Tarantino and the gang perfected an entire monologue about the gay subtext behind *Top Gun*, something he replayed for his cameo in the indie movie *Sleep With Me*. It is not know whether he and Scott ever discussed the matter.

**Above right:** Given his history with huge commercial hits such as *Top Gun*, with Tom Cruise, British director Tony Scott seemed an unlikely choice to helm *True Romance*. But after Tarantino sent him the script through a mutual contact, like so many before him Scott was captivated.

Thus, he and Roger Avary, now writing partners, concocted a plan to fund *True Romance* as the Coen brothers had *Blood Simple*, raising the budget piecemeal via rich investors. They would shoot it for $60,000 on 16mm, and make their mark. With Los Angeles too full of film people to pay heed to another pair of needy kids with a script, they got nowhere.

After four years of the Hollywood high hat, it fell into the hands of an inexperienced producer named Stanley Margolis. Blown away by the scandalous opening pages, he pursued a budget of $2.7 million, obligingly mortgaging his house, before plunging into a labyrinth of potential backers, rum deals and finally lawsuits (ownership became uncertain). With Tarantino directing *Reservoir Dogs*, Scott Spiegel recommended Bill Lustig as a replacement, a director best known for the schlocky thriller *Maniac*

*Cop*. Tarantino liked him, liked his movie, thought he might give *True Romance* a gust of cheap, exploitative mayhem. But Lustig fell out of favour when he suggested a more upbeat ending might help sell the picture – per Tarantino's draft, Clarence ends up with his brains blown out.

Tarantino did not take lightly to anyone messing with his scripts.

In December 1991, it was announced in industry bible *Variety* that Tony Scott, no less, the British director behind such commercial behemoths as *Top Gun* and *Days of Thunder* (a Tarantino favourite), would direct *True Romance*. After Tarantino had discovered a mutual contact, Scott had read both *Reservoir Dogs* and *True Romance* back to back at 4a.m., the firefly sprawl of LA providing the perfect backdrop. He was mesmerized by the dialogue; it was like a new kind of poetry of the streets. He was on the phone the next morning, 'I want to do both these movies'[5].

With the former earmarked for its author, it was the tale of Clarence and Alabama, Tarantino's love story, he would create. With Scott came Warner Brothers and a budget of $13 million ($5 million more than that of *Pulp Fiction*). Miramax had attempted to gazump the studio with a last-minute deal where James Foley would direct on a budget of $7 million, but succumbed to a piece of the Warner-Scott deal. Tarantino ended up with $40,000.

There was a brief period when Scott considered only producing the film, leaving it open for Tarantino to direct. Following *Reservoir Dogs*, he would be offered the chance to direct each of his early screenplays, only to decline. His response was unsentimental, they had been written to be his first film; he didn't want to go backwards. A Tarantinoesque metaphor came to mind: 'I think of them as like old girlfriends, but I didn't want to marry them anymore.'[6]

**Right:** Patricia Arquette (Alabama) and Christian Slater (Clarence) pose for a famous publicity shot. Establishing that Clarence was an alter ego of the writer, during rehearsals Slater spent a day with Quentin Tarantino to see what he was like. Eventually, Scott and Slater would decide to make Clarence mellower than his real-life inspiration.

In any case, the chance to see his world through Scott's eyes was too enticing. Scott considered *True Romance* among his best work. While it has Tarantino's guts, it has Scott's heartbeat: slick and frenetic. Starring Christian Slater as a bright-eyed Clarence (more movie star than geek) and Patricia Arquette as a perky, loveable Alabama. It is Alabama who provides a dotted line to *Reservoir Dogs* – she is recalled by Mr. White when talking to Joe Cabot. 'To me they are all living in this one universe,'[7] explained Tarantino.

The gaggle of supporting characters sees the debut of Samuel L. Jackson, albeit briefly, in the Tarantino universe. The same goes for another later leading man, Brad Pitt, as a bong-chugging loafer, virtually moulded to the sofa, transfixed by the television.

Scott added the fairy-tale veneer. He saw Tarantino as a true romantic and Alabama his dream girl (she willingly submits to those Chiba movies). Ironically, Scott also stuck with Lustig's happy ending.

'We got together and talked about it,' recalled Tarantino, who found himself unperturbed when Scott also straightened out the chronology. 'Tony said he wanted to change the ending, not for commercial reasons, but because he really liked these kids and wanted to see them to get away.'[8]

The film's most memorable moment returns us to Tarantino's dark arts. Herein Dennis Hopper, as Clarence's estranged but loyal pop Cliff, jibes Christopher Walken's preened Sicilian mobster Coccotti into shooting him. Two seasoned actors going toe-to-toe, cut beautifully to the rhythm of performance.

**Right:** Despite the backing of a major studio, good reviews, and a huge budget compared to the $60,000 Quentin Tarantino had hoped to make it for, the film still failed to find much of an audience

christian slater   patricia arquette

STEALING
CHEATING
KILLING

WHO SAYS ROMANCE IS DEAD?

A TONY SCOTT FILM

# TRUE
# romance

dennis hopper   val kilmer   gary oldman
brad pitt   christopher walken

Hopper's retired cop countering his foe's deathly-serene interrogation methods – finessing an old Video Archives routine – with the news that, historically speaking, Sicilians were 'spawned by niggers'[9] (it all goes back to the Moors). The magic is watching Walken's icy demeanour slowly crack. 'I haven't killed anybody since 1984,'[10] he barks, regaining his composure, a bullet in Cliff's brain. The scene is so funny because of what it is daring. Nevertheless, it wouldn't be last time Tarantino's unflinching vernacular ran into controversy.

With his unique delivery – a former hoofer, he almost tap-dances through his lines – Walken proved a virtuoso with Tarantino's argot. For a brief while Tarantino had enlisted Walken as Mr. Blonde in *Reservoir Dogs* until scheduling conflicts postponed his arrival until *True Romance* and then *Pulp Fiction*. The latter granted him a single magnificent monologue, delivered with all of Walken's jazzy syncopations, in which he regales the young Butch with the story of his father's hidden watch.

While held in high regard by Tarantino, *True Romance* failed at the box office, making little over $12 million. The arthouse crowd may have suspected the shimmer of Hollywood as a sell-out. Mainstream audiences were not yet attuned to Tarantino's scapegrace storytelling. It would take *Pulp Fiction* to kick that door down.

**Above:** Quentin Tarantino claims the confrontation between Hopper's security guard and Christopher Walken's mafioso Vincenzo Coccotti as one of his proudest moments. It was adapted from a speech a black friend of his mother's had made while staying at their house.

**Opposite:** Clifford Worley (Dennis Hopper) coolly meets his end. Hopper fell in love with Tarantino's language, which he didn't see as necessarily offensive, but rather a true evocation of the culture. They didn't meet until after the movie, when they ended up standing alongside one another at the urinals at a nightclub opening.

**Above:** The violence in *True Romance* added to Quentin Tarantino's growing reputation as a divisive figure, especially the shocking brutality meted out to Alabama. But Patricia Arquette vehemently defended the film. If you're looking for a hero, she fumed, don't come to this movie.

**Opposite above:** Dick (Michael Rapaport) and his stoner flatmate Floyd (Brad Pitt) provide a Los Angeles base for Clarence's drug deal. This is evidently a cut scene, as in the finished fim, in accordance with Pitt's idea for the character, we never see Floyd leave the sofa.

**Opposite below:** The case in point: Pitt's immortal Floyd seen in his natural habitat. This hilarious stoner cameo marks the superstar's debut in the Tarantino universe. He would follow the role by working directly for the auteur in *Inglorious Basterds* and *Once Upon a Time in Hollywood*.

# 'Tony said he wanted to change the ending, not for commercial reasons, but because he really liked these kids and wanted to see them to get away.'

*– Quentin Tarantino*

*Natural Born Killers* was Tarantino's second attempt at a first film. But where *True Romance* became the adaption he embraced, this was the former 'girlfriend' he publicly scorned, accepting only a story-by credit as he sought to distance himself from what he considered a personal insult. He has consciously refused to watch Oliver Stone's reworking of his script; promising only that one day he might catch it on hotel pay per view.

Before it burst into notoriety, *Natural Born Killers* had ingeniously existed within *True Romance* as the script Clarence is writing. Metafictionally, it tells the story of telling the story of Mickey and Mallory, loved-up serial killers, apprehended after a murder spree down Highway 58. They are now coveted by bottom-feeding television personality Wayne Gale and his 'American Maniacs' show, a character cut from the cloth of Geraldo Rivera, the real-life attorney turned talk-show host who once interviewed Charles Manson.

Proposed as a stand-alone script, Tarantino collaborated with another Video Archivist – Rand Vossler, one of his closest friends. Vossler had actually beaten Tarantino into the business, albeit as a 'feature development guy'[11] at MGM, which Tarantino naturally spied as a potential avenue for getting the film off the ground. MGM, however, were utterly bemused by what they read, leaving Vossler to quit his job and form a company with his friend – Natural Born Filmmakers. It was a deal not so different from the casual nature of his partnership with Lawrence Bender – but this time the loose-limbed approach to legal documentation would have repercussions.

In the afterglow of his success, Tarantino's agent often had to clear up the mess of promises made that he could

never keep. He had to learn to keep his distance. Even from his friends.

Vossler was one who would go down in the waves.

As with *True Romance*, there was no interest at first, leaving Tarantino to beg shifts at Video Archives to stay afloat. Once he had met Bender, and *Reservoir Dogs* gathered pace, Vossler was largely left to his own devices. As a parting gift, Tarantino offered the script to Vossler to direct himself for $1 if he could get funding. Unwittingly this kicked off a chain reaction that would lead the film towards both Stone and the courts. Bullish young producers Jane Hamsher and Don Murphy came onboard, claiming they could raise $500,000 for Vossler. They were soon taking meetings without him in the room, and it became increasingly clear that his presence was stifling any deal. Isolated, broke and a little desperate, Vossler accepted a deal to take his name off the film as director. He claimed, naively, that the money would be used for him to shoot a 'calling card' segment of the

**Above:** Oliver Stone on the set of *Natural Born Killers*. While he liked the script, Stone never bought into the growing cult surrounding Quentin Tarantino and felt he was perfectly within his rights to make substantial changes to the original script.

**Opposite:** A posed publicity shot of serial killer couple Mallory (Juliette Lewis) and Mickey (Woody Harrelson) from *Natural Born Killers*. Amid all the murder and mayhem of his story, Tarantino originally conceived the film as another classic love story.

script to convince financiers what he was still capable of doing.

Two days later, he was fired from the project entirely. He immediately sued Hamsher and Murphy. Tarantino was furious, insisting that the deal they had struck had been dependent on Vossler making the film guerrilla-style for $30,000, never as some big production. If Hamsher and Murphy were going after bigger money, then he wanted a bigger share. Vossler would eventually be paid off and silenced, his friendship with Tarantino in tatters.

Worse was to come.

**Below:** A posed publicity shot of serial killer couple Mallory (Juliette Lewis) and Mickey (Woody Harrelson) from *Natural Born Killers*. Amid all the murder and mayhem of his story, Tarantino originally conceived the film as another classic love story.

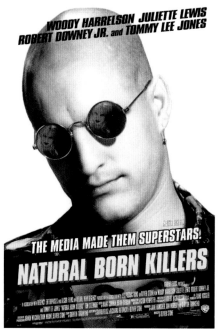

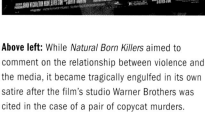

**Above left:** While *Natural Born Killers* aimed to comment on the relationship between violence and the media, it became tragically engulfed in its own satire after the film's studio Warner Brothers was cited in the case of a pair of copycat murders.

**Above right:** Death becomes them – in Stone's eyes Mallory (Juliette Lewis) and Mickey (Woody Harrelson) were the new Bonnie and Clyde, and his wild editing approach was heavily influenced by the Warren Beatty-Faye Dunaway classic.

As *Reservoir Dogs* gathered steam, so did *Natural Born Killers*, interesting the likes of Sean Penn, Brian De Palma and David Fincher. News of Tarantino's audacious talent was beginning to spread. Stone had heard about the script at a Hollywood party, getting hold of a copy he was impressed enough to buy it.

Coming off the back of *Heaven and Earth*, the third of his Vietnam trilogy, he was in the mood to make a crime film. Something akin to the scripts he had written as a young man for *Scarface* and *Year of the Dragon*.

Tarantino's script didn't wholly suit Stone's purposes. It was too Roger Corman: clearly a first film, and contained within a movie-movie world of Tarantino's devising. Stone wanted to throw it at the real world; to capture what he saw as the 'apocalyptic feeling that we get from society'[12]. He wanted

to probe our relationship with violence, with television, and the media as a whole in the early 1990s. Later, the very fact it was based on a story by Tarantino would add another layer to its dizzyingly ironic scheme. By then, Tarantino was boxed as the dark side of Hollywood, purveyor of hip ultraviolence – the very theme Stone was throwing into his philosophical blender.

In short, Stone wanted to make it an Oliver Stone film. He pushed Wayne Gale (Robert Downey Jr.) and the media frenzy to the side, adding a grotesque backstory for Mickey (Woody Harrelson incandescent as a shaven-headed demon) and Mallory (a caterwauling, beanpole Juliette Lewis) as a canned American sitcom called 'I love Mallory' (an ugly distortion of Tarantino's pop-cultural tangents), as well as flights of Native American mumbo-jumbo suggesting cycles of violence bequeathed through time.

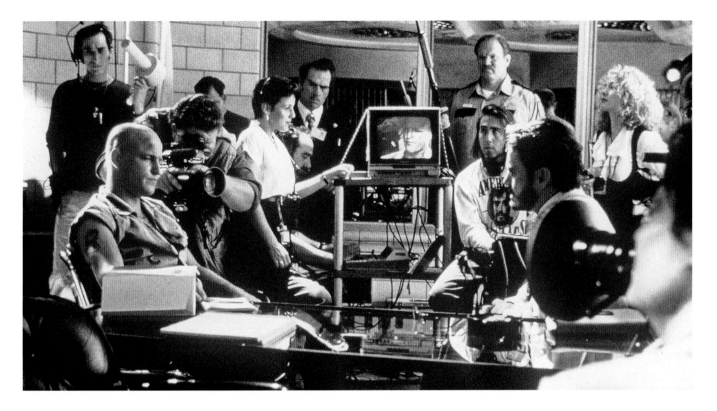

After fifty-six days of shooting, and eleven months of editing, the resulting blizzard of different film stocks, images of despots beamed onto shopping mall walls (Stone's socio-political connectivity) and choreographed depravity fell squarely into the love-it-or-hate-it category. Critics were equally divided: it was either a transcendent dissection of modern ills, or a gabble of half-crazed ideas and lurid bloodletting. It was all gesture, all style, but powerful in its own stubborn way. And doubling down on its own irony, it was banned wholesale for months in the UK, before the BBFC came to their senses. Hitting American cinemas in the summer of 1994, only months before *Pulp Fiction*, its notoriety brought it $50 million in the US (on a budget of $34 million).

Tarantino reacted with righteous fury. He called the appropriation of the script by Hamsher and Murphy, 'skulduggerous theft'[13]. He publicly washed his hands of it, which Stone considered very bad sport. It was a 'samurai code'[14] that a writer live with a director's choices. 'If you go to film school,' he shot back, 'film school teaches you a certain amount of humility.'[15]

Besides, he estimated Tarantino was paid $400,000 for his troubles (they have since, reputedly, made up over a night of board games).

Surveying the original script, it is arguably the most lucid and political of all Tarantino's early work. He may have skipped college, but here is the broad spectrum of his knowledge and feel for modern America. Having landed an interview with Mickey, Gale boasts of the magnitude of its import, the words pouring straight out of the reference library of Tarantino's febrile mind: '…This is the tearful reporting of the Hindenburg disaster, this is Truffaut setting the record straight on Hitchcock, this is a Robert Capa photo, this is Woodward and Bernstein meeting Deep Throat in an underground parking lot …'[16]

This is the one that got away.

**Above:** Australian TV shock merchant Wayne Gale (Robert Downey Jr. right) interviews Mickey (Harrelson). In the low-budget version he had once contemplated making, Tarantino had earmarked the part of Gale for himself.

**Above:** During the making of *From Dusk Till Dawn*, director Robert Rodriguez takes a musical interlude outside the set of vampire den, the Titty Twister. The versatile Texan-born director, who would find a kindred spirit in Tarantino, was so obsessed with becoming a director he used to deliver his homework as short films made with the family camcorder.

It was that tireless networker Scott Spiegel who first introduced Tarantino to Bob Kurtzman of KNB, the special effects company he ran with his partners Greg Nicotero and Howard Berger. They had provided all the demonic oozing for Sam Raimi's *Evil Dead 2* as well as dead buffalos

for Kevin Costner's Oscar-winning Western *Dances with Wolves*. Kurtzman was another industry tenderfoot with an eye on directing. He already had a 20-page treatment for *From Dusk Till Dawn*, a genre-splicing 'gangster-vampire'[17] movie. The basics were in place: the Titty Twister, the Tex-Mex bordello that provides cover for a coven of vampires, the bank-robbing Gecko brothers, the troubled preacher and his kids. Kurtzman was in need of a writer to expand it into a script he could legitimately pitch as his directing debut.

The next day, a parcel arrived on his desk, containing a sample of the prospective writer's work in the shape of two scripts. He opened the first, entitled *True Romance*, and

began to read and that was that. He could return to read *Natural Born Killers* at his leisure. Kurtzman is fairly certain that he was the first to professionally commission Tarantino, who returned within weeks with an 88-page script.

This first draft, Tarantino would admit, was designed to meet the billing of a cheap exploitation movie. By his standards, the characters were one-dimensional, the plotting formulaic. 'The whole thing was set up as a showcase for KNB make-up effects,'[18] he insisted, but there was no missing the bravura dialogue, percussive violence and hip movie references. He couldn't help being himself. The preacher and his family are named the

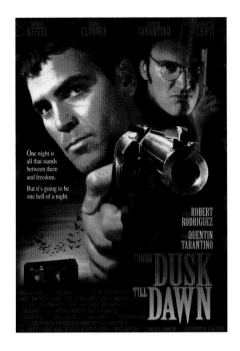

**Above left:** The name of the film was inspired by the signs outside drive-in movie theatres that promised to run films non-stop throughout the night no matter what the quality.

**Above right:** The film's notorious Gecko brothers, psychotic Richie (Quentin Tarantino) and his protective elder sibling Seth (George Clooney). While ostensibly a horror movie, Tarantino loved the idea of concealing its true identity in the crime story of these bank-robbing brothers on the run to Mexico.

Fullers after director Sam Fuller, while the expansion of the front half of the story had been modelled on Jim Thompson's novel *The Getaway*. 'Instead of two lovers it was two brothers,'[19] he explained proudly. Kurtzman's initial treatment had only devoted about four paragraphs to events prior to the horror of the Titty Twister. Tarantino wanted to hide the vampires in a suspense movie about these bank-robbing siblings without any foreshadowing of the horror to come. It would be the most abrupt collision between the real and generic in his entire career.

All Kurtzman could offer was a meagre $1,500, knowing the quality of the writing was worth far more. As some recompense, he would offer his crew gratis on *Reservoir Dogs*, and KNB would create Officer Marvin Nash's severed ear and mutilated face, the samurai sword wounds in *Pulp Fiction* and a severed finger for *Four Rooms*. However, even armed with Tarantino's script, Kurtzman got no traction while he remained as the named director.

Tarantino had met Robert Rodriguez at the Toronto Film Festival, where they shared a young directors panel. Based in Austin, Texas, Rodriguez had caused a stir with his Texican gangland thriller *El Mariachi*; made, he claimed, for $7,000, $2,000 of which had been raised by offering himself as a lab rat for a cholesterol-busting drug. He and Tarantino shared the same religious devotion to movies.

Scanning the printed bios provided for the directors sharing the stage, Rodriguez was struck by the mention of an unmade Tarantino script: a border-town vampire movie. 'It's two movies for the price of one,'[20] quipped the author. You could argue it is three films for the price of one: the added colour being a serial killer flick, in which the dangerously child-like Richie Gecko's psychotic impulses threaten to spin out of control.

Having turned down Kurtzman's offer to sell the screenplay back to him to direct – he had no interest in dancing with an old girlfriend – Rodriguez encouraged Tarantino that he might like to direct under the proviso he did a second draft, thickening up the characters, refreshing the dialogue, including Cheech Marin's cannonade barker. The ongoing bromance would include Rodriguez directing a segment of *Four Rooms*, Tarantino taking a cameo in his *El Mariachi* reboot *Desperado*, Rodriguez helping score sections of *Pulp Fiction*, Tarantino directing a single scene of *Sin City*, and the pair teaming on their foolhardy Grindhouse extravaganza.

First, though, came the mixed blessing of *From Dusk Till Dawn*. Backed by Miramax to the tune of $19 million, and released in January 1996, the studio saw it as an unexpected bonus – an interim splash of Tarantino between *Pulp Fiction* and *Jackie Brown*. Rodriguez and Tarantino now had enough clout to land themselves backend deals, with Lawrence Bender also guaranteed as producer. The whole project came together a little too quickly.

An added enticement for Tarantino was the chance to take his first leading role as the deranged Richie Gecko, sotto voce psycho to George Clooney's more straightforwardly crooked Seth (there are echoes of Mr. Blonde and his professional cohorts in *Reservoir Dogs*: the Geckos even don black suits).

Returning to the script he could put meat on the bones of a role he was going to play. He hadn't written Richie for himself as he had Clarence, Wayne Gale and Mr. Pink). He hadn't been visualizing anyone for the film; this was simply, 'A head-banging horror film for horror film lovers.'[21] A friend had once described horror as the heavy metal of film, and the description had stuck. He confidently expected horror fans to see it six times.

On that level, it was a fulfilling experience. Clooney, he said, became like a brother. John Travolta had been offered Seth (as had Steven Buscemi, Michael Madsen and Tim Roth), but scheduling clashes denied us an intriguing post-*Pulp Fiction* double act. There was no residual bitterness towards Juliette Lewis although she had played Mallory in *Natural Born Killers*. Tarantino actively pursued her to play the greatly expanded role of the (at first) demure Kate Fuller. They were good friends, and he liked the idea of cutting against the grain of Lewis' edgy resumé. He especially enjoyed the confrontations with Harvey Keitel as Jacob Fuller, the priest wrestling with a crisis of faith.

Meanwhile, Tarantino went Method. 'Quentin was never on set,' he said, 'it was always Richie Gecko.'[22]

The film that emerged was, as promised, head banging and genre bending, but it felt like faux-Tarantino. The engorged third act is especially campy, with the protagonists confronting hordes of vampires in the bowels of the Titty Twister. These were vampires Quentin-style: none of that antique soul-searching about living forever. No, he exclaimed, 'They're just a bunch of carnivorous, banshee beasts.'[23] The result is onrush of limb-lopping slaughter (with KNB using green blood to swerve ratings issues), lumpen humour and the odd eccentric snarl of excitement.

**Above:** The vampires of *From Dusk Till Dawn* were not of the classical, dapper variety, but carnivorous grotesques created by the special effects experts KNB. In fact, the film had originally been conceived as a low-budget schlocker to show off the company's facility with prosthetics.

**Opposite:** Quentin Tarantino still considers the unnervingly placid psycho Richie Gecko to be his finest performance as an actor. He relished the chance to concentrate entirely on acting, staying in character for the entire shoot.

**Right:** Salma Hayek's vampiric table dancer Santanico Pandemonium was named after a Mexican horror movie Tarantino had seen in his Video Archives days. Hayek, who was terrified of snakes, claims she had to go into a trance in order to complete the scene with the albino python.

At $26 million, the box office returns were underwhelming; it did indeed play to the horror fan, but no one else.

There were critics who bought into its trashy vulgarity. *Entertainment Weekly*'s Owen Gleiberman cutely thought the combo of styles was like merging two movies from opposite sides of the video store, but noted that 'it begins as a movie and devolves into a pseudo-movie'. It was just a gross-out, and Tarantino had never been that. Had he and Rodriguez brought out the worst tendencies in one another?

Tarantino's acting was still a matter of debate. So much so, it was almost a *bête noire*: the boy genius' fatal flaw, this entrenched desire to act (to be loved, some suspected). The irony was delicious, a director who wanted to act! 'A lot of critics resent me for trying this route,'[24] he reflected. He felt that Richie Gecko was a breakthrough. This was the longest and deepest he had been inside one of his characters.

Indeed, Richie is the most interesting thing in the film. Tarantino manages to subdue all that natural puppy-dog energy, although it keeps threatening to well up. He is genuinely discomforting. The geek with a split personality, like Anthony Perkins as Norman Bates, and the cracked glasses of Dustin Hoffman in *Straw Dogs*. You miss his skittish sociopath once he's been transformed into a demonic distortion of that now familiar Tarantino face. The film has an excitable, nervous energy: the killers, the loot, the kidnapped family and the backchat. It is crossing the border into horror that undoes it.

Tarantino was unrepentant. 'It doesn't matter to me if critics look at it like a celebrity turn.'[25] Hadn't Spielberg told him that in *Desperado* (in which he delivered an elaborate bar-room joke) he was a 'cinema raconteur'[26]?

Acting, he insisted more than once, taught him everything he knew about directing. There were many different Tarantinos clamouring to be heard. The actor, the writer, the director and the stand-up comedian who could show off on talk shows. And, he added, 'I have a critic guy inside me.'[27]

Tarantino is a rare bird indeed, a director inspired by reading movie critics, not ignoring them. After *Reservoir Dogs'* debut in Sundance, he had made a point of getting personally acquainted with all the chief American critics. The serious critics, he would insist, not the online blowhards that swarmed on the internet. Tarantino cites Pauline Kael, the doyenne of the American critical scene through the 1960s and '70s, as one of the biggest influences on his career.

By the time of *Inglourious Basterds*, Michael Fassbender's Lt Archie Hicox has a backstory as a former critic, who has written a 'subtextual film criticism study of the work of German director G.W. Pabst.'[28]

Tarantino even mines his own of vein of critical thinking, writing extensive pieces on whatever stirs his interest. Material he may publish some day. Typically, he rarely follows the consensus. He once contemplated offering academically minded journal *Film Comment* an article 'in complete and utter defence of *Showgirls*.'[29]

**Left:** While Tarantino was still mulling over what to direct next after the triumph of *Pulp Fiction*, independent studio Miramax took full advantage of his burgeoning celebrity by marketing *From Dusk Till Dawn* as an interim burst of Tarantino cool that just happened to be a horror flick.

# 'MY CHARACTERS NEVER STOP TELLING STORIES...'

## Pulp Fiction

The second film by Quentin Tarantino began life, like the first, as a concept dreamed up in his Video Archives days. Parts of it had been written alongside (and at times within) *True Romance*, only to be set aside and allowed to simmer in his imagination while he made his impressive debut with *Reservoir Dogs*.

'Everything I have written,' he confessed, 'has at least twenty pages that are taken from other things I've done.'[1] The plan was an anthology movie like Mario Bava's 1963 horror triptych *Black Sabbath*, but inspired by Tarantino's love of old crime magazines like *Black Mask*. The legendary periodical was home to Raymond Chandler and Dashiell Hammett and more modern, hardboiled writers like Elmore Leonard and Jim Thompson – who once qualified as pulp but had crashed the literary party, just as he had duped the bouncers of the arthouse scene.

An anthology of crime shorts, Tarantino originally reasoned, was another cost effective away of getting a film off the ground. He could shoot one, and then raise the money for the next. 'I would keep building on it until it was a feature.'[2]

*Pulp Fiction* would evolve into something more ingenious. Three interlinked Los Angeles crime stories that switch back and forth in time like the dial of a radio being tuned in and out of different stations. The idea had come to him while in the edit room on *Reservoir Dogs* (and *Pulp Fiction* is nothing if not also a commentary on film editing). Here were the different chapters of his debut film only running in wild zigzags. It is the mood that flows chronologically. Thus we can witness the ignominious death of John Travolta's louche but lovable hitman Vincent as he exits the toilet (reading pulpy spy thriller *Modesty Blaise*), only for him to return, right as rain, and triumphantly saunter out of the film, automatic lodged into the waistband of his (actually Jimmie's) shorts.

In plot terms, the time-warping framework made the film thrillingly unpredictable; *Pulp Fiction* refuses to behave like a regular movie.

**Above:** Quentin Tarantino showing off the trademark quiff of his younger years. Much of the concept for *Pulp Fiction* was already written by the time he completed *Reservoir Dogs*, but it was the influence of travelling in Europe for the first time that would completely transform the script. Suddenly it became very personal.

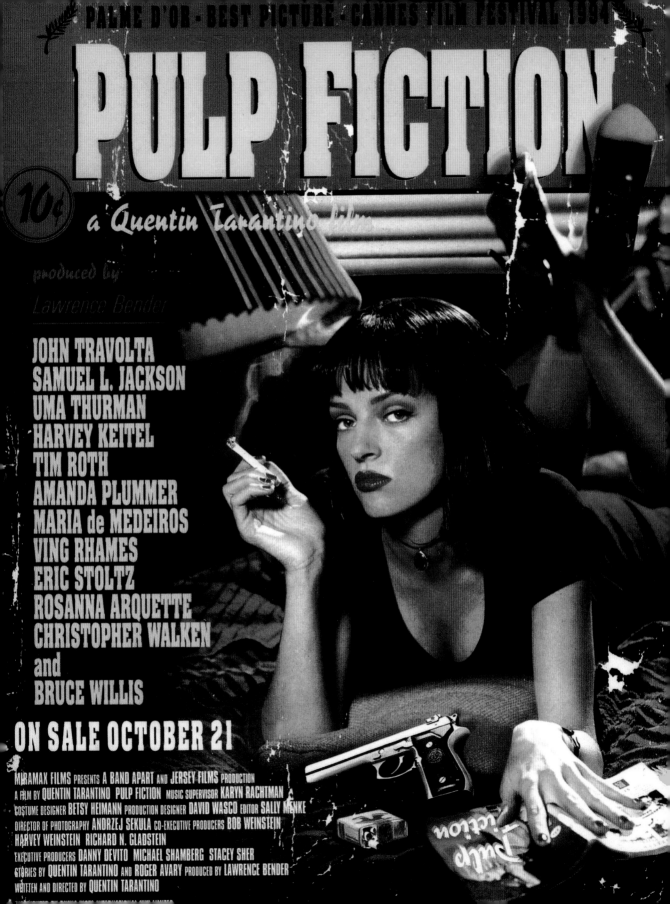

This was never about Tarantino showing off his big brain, or being a wiseguy. He was once again applying a novelist's freedoms to cinema. If a story demanded to be told in a linear fashion, then that is exactly how he would tell it. 'But the glory,' he grinned, 'is in pulling it off my way.'[3]

After a year on the road promoting *Reservoir Dogs*, it had been time to go to work. He had recently signed a $1 million development deal with Danny DeVito's Jersey Films, which in turn worked out of the major studio TriStar (a constituency of Sony). As well as a fine comic actor, DeVito was a canny producer on the indie scene who sufficiently appreciated the rich, radical voice of *Reservoir Dogs* (he had read the script during Lawrence Bender's early overtures) to offer the young filmmaker a home for his next venture. Tarantino would return with arguably his masterpiece.

The three parts of his conjoined trilogy were to be contemporary twists on classic underworld fables – the kind you've seen 'a zillion times'[4] – populated with a sprawling ensemble of criminals, molls, boxers and assorted victims. In the first, a pair of hitmen are sent to retrieve a stolen briefcase. Exactly the kind of pre-Credits gun-popping set-up you get in a Schwarzenegger movie. Only we'll spend more time simply hanging out with the mishap-prone pair before and after the hit. In the second, one of these hitmen is assigned to keep the wife of his mobster boss entertained for the night while he is out of town. No funny business. Of course, there will be funny business, but not the kind we expect. For a time, the post-heist mayhem of *Reservoir Dogs* had been the third tale, before it took on a life of its own. Conceptually, *Pulp Fiction* predated *Reservoir Dogs*.

Instead, Tarantino persuaded fellow Video Archivist Roger Avary to allow him to lift the bones of another his scripts. Written under the grandiose title *Pandemonium Reigns* it depicted what befalls a prizefighter when he elects not to throw a fight as agreed.

Despite the LA setting, noir roots and the dime store tang of its title, *Pulp Fiction* was to be Tarantino's homage to the narrative wiles of Jean-Luc Godard, chief rule-breaker of the French New Wave. The production company he had formed with Bender was named A Band Apart as a tip of the hat to Godard's rearrangement of gangster tropes in *Bande à part*. Tarantino wasn't riffing on American crime movies so much as French riffs on American crime movies. That he reworked most of the screenplay while on a three-month sabbatical in Amsterdam only added to the feeling of a seedy Los Angeles infused with European sophistication.

He chose an apartment in Amsterdam largely because of the vibe. You could drink beer in movie theatres and smoke a joint in a café. Plus, there was a Howard Hawks festival in town, which he imbibed like a drug. On the opening page of *Pulp Fiction* he describes two characters talking in a 'rapid-fire motion, like in *His Girl Friday*'[5], Hawks' 1940 comedy classic.

For a few weeks Avary joined him to help adapt the *Pandemonium Reigns* section. According to Tarantino they went back to their files of ideas, pulling out the best scenes, and spreading them over the floor to start lining them up. They used Tarantino's computer to begin putting it all together. Originally, said Avary, 'the agreement was that we would split the writing part and the back end participation.'[6] Exactly what contribution Avary made to the final screenplay really depended on who you asked. In any case, he departed to make *Killing Zoe*, an unsatisfying heist thriller with Eric Stolz and Julie Delpy, to which Tarantino had generously lent his by now influential name.

Life inevitably began to bleed into fiction. So Travolta's chilled Vincent regales his partner Jules (Samuel L. Jackson) with the idiosyncrasies of European burger nomenclature. Vincent has recently returned from a sojourn in, yes, Amsterdam (while never explained, Tarantino conceived of him running a foreign club for Ving Rhames' crime boss Marsellus).

When rakish clean-up specialist Winston Wolfe (a return for Harvey Keitel) accepts a coffee from the pouting Jimmie (played by Tarantino to a mixed reception), he asks for lots of cream, lots of sugar: exactly how Tarantino likes it. *The New Yorker* once referred to him as the 'junk food Proust'[7], or words to that effect. This concentration on the rituals of food and drink, the glories of a 'five-dollar shake'[8], the repeated motif of breakfast cereals (on which the fledgling writer subsisted) or the ethics of paying a tip are all part of fleshy details with which Tarantino spiked old genres.

What began in *Reservoir Dogs* with a coffee shop discussion of Madonna's virtue is now a symphony of distractions, gags, pop

cultural meanderings and a whole lot of talk. 'My characters never stop telling stories,'[9] he laughed.

Where traditional (square) thrillers fret over exposition, Tarantino riffed in ephemeral grooves on blueberry pancakes or the ethics of a foot massage. Counterintuitively the effect is thrilling – the characters unfurl into poignant and farcical human dimensions. These were movie people behaving like real people.

During his (self) promotional travels, Tarantino had landed at a Spanish Film Festival where Tim Roth was a fellow guest. Into the early hours, Tarantino would call his hotel and read him pages from the unfinished script, promising the actor he would be involved. The matter was settled when Roth suggested he also cast Amanda Plummer. Roth had done a student film with the jittery, bird-like actor and was

keen to work with her again. But she had to have a gun in her hand, he laughed. 'I can think of nothing more dangerous than Amanda Plummer with a gun,'[10] Roth later explained. And lo, petty hold-up merchants and loved-up twosome Pumpkin and Honey Bunny were born.

When Tarantino announced he wished to keep his budget down to $8 million, TriStar began to cool on the project. It was the perverse side of Hollywood that Tarantino never understood: 'They would rather have me come to them with a star-

driven piece of material that they could do for $25 million.'[11] They weren't looking for hip they wanted a hit. They didn't see how a close-up of a guy shooting up was supposed to get laughs.

Tarantino turned instead to his partners at Miramax, where Richard Gladstein had recently been installed as head of production. Through Bender, Gladstein secured an early read of the script, and knew the jangling claustrophobia of *Reservoir Dogs* had expanded into something operatic. Miramax considered $8 million a bargain.

That was when Tarantino threw them a curveball. He wanted Travolta to play Vincent, one of his leads. To put it lightly, Travolta's career was on the skids. He was wealthy enough, but the glory days of *Saturday Night Fever*, *Blow Out* and *Urban Cowboy* were distant memories. He was reduced to talking baby movies, while rivals such as Tom Hanks and Kevin Costner made hay.

As far as Tarantino was concerned, if he could reinvigorate the textures and plots of old genres and lost movies, then he could reinvent washed-up stars as leading men. It would become a form of meta-motif.

At Tarantino's bidding, they had already met. At the time, he wasn't really thinking of Travolta for *Pulp Fiction*. Settling down to play board games at Tarantino's messy, memorabilia-strewn West Hollywood apartment – by astonishing coincidence, the same address Travolta had rented back

in the 1970s – he mentioned a horror movie he had written called *From Dusk Till Dawn*. But Tarantino mostly waxed lyrical about his guest's vaunted career, and its decline: 'Don't you know what you mean to the American cinema?'[12]

Travolta returned home, confused, berated but strangely touched by Tarantino's belief in him. A few weeks later the script for *Pulp Fiction* arrived, with a note attached: 'Look at Vincent'. The director had been thinking of offering the part to Michael Madsen as a possible return (from the dead) for *Reservoir Dogs'* Vic Vega. Madsen, to his eternal dismay, was lassoed in the shoot for Costner's languorous Western *Wyatt Earp* and had to pass. So his friend turned the character into Vic's brother Vincent (for a long while a *Vega Brothers* movie was on the cards) and put it to Travolta.

Miramax, meanwhile, expressed their doubts. Travolta? He was toxic. They were leaning towards Daniel Day-Lewis. Tarantino stood firm. In his head, Vincent was now permanently blessed with Travolta's dewy eyes and sleepy smile. As with the ear slicing, his resolve was uncrackable. Unfathomably, Travolta then expressed what he called 'moral doubts'[13]. He knew the writing was sensational, but it took all of Tarantino's persuasive powers to convince a proud family man that the free-wheeling profanity, casual deaths and poeticized glimpses of shooting up were simply textures of the morally inverted, snow-globe movie-mythology he was building.

What a god of casting Tarantino truly is: blending our sense of Travolta into the character, the line between life and movie, movie and life remaining elusive. Travolta plays Vincent as a hitman who is kind of like John Travolta. This was less a rebirth than a revamp. The sexy idol of the 1970s had slackened into a middle-age paunch, jowls and a lived-in complexion, but he was still unmistakable. As Tarantino foretold, talent hadn't departed, it had simply lain dormant, and Travolta is a wonder to behold. His smoothly sidling walk, his double takes, his unruly forelock: he personifies *Pulp Fiction*'s amoral persona – the lovable killer with the flicker of panic in his blue eyes. Vincent is no dope either; he reveals an enquiring mind that Tarantino had modelled on Travolta himself. He even gets to dance.

Jack Rabbit Slim's is the slick 1950s-style burger joint like a pop art explosion with its convertible-shaped booths and peroxide blonde Monroe. All the waiters and waitresses dress as dead stars (Steve Buscemi cameos as an ersatz Buddy Holly). It was partly based on the nightclub in the Elvis stock-car musical *Speedway* with its racing motifs – the dance floor is a speedometer. 'I threw in little things, as if I was running a restaurant,'[14] enthused Tarantino.

The twist contest was another tribute to Godard and Anna Karina's cool-cat dancing in *Bande à part*. On set it was Tarantino who demonstrated the moves to Travolta, slipping off his shoes and beginning to twist to Chuck Berry's 'You Never Can Tell'. 'It was like watching a twelve-year-old at his first dance,'[15] the actor laughed. Travolta projected Vincent onto his corny shapes, 'someone who is on heroin, who's a little overweight, who refers to the novelty dances of sixties when he grew up.'[16]

And yet there is no missing the fluid grace of a natural, the ironic gesture towards movie history. Tarantino knew, and it was as if Mia knew too, we wanted to see him dance, to show that swagger. The movie is

**Opposite:** The immortal Honey Bunny (Amanda Plummer) and Pumpkin (Tim Roth) hatching a plan to hold up the diner. Created late in the writing process, this highly-strung Bonnie and Clyde were specifically modelled on the combination of the two actors who were cast to play them.

**Right:** Butch (Bruce Willis) on Z's stolen chopper. Not a motorbike, a chopper. While writing the part of the absconding boxer, Tarantino can never have imagined he would land a star of Willis' calibre, but he came to love how he embodied an old-school film noir heavy with a heart.

almost, but not quite, getting carried away with its own pop delirium.

As the edgily flirtatious, Louise Brooks-fringed Mia, it was Uma Thurman's strange gangly limbs and long fingers that Tarantino took delight in. He had a thing for her hands and especially her feet, which he felt were unique. Tarantino had told Thurman he wanted attitude (bizarrely fixing on Eva Gabor's animated cat in Disney's *The Aristocats*), and as they danced he called out the required move: the Catwoman, the hitchhiker, the Watusi, the swim … He took over the handheld camera, and began to dance along with them. Even as it fades out all too soon, the scene twists into the very celluloid immortality evoked by Jack Rabbit Slim's.

Then relatively unknown, Thurman was another example of Tarantino's virtuoso casting. 'I talked to damn nearly every actress in Hollywood about the Mia role, with the idea that when I met Mia, I'd know it,' he recalled (Rosanna Arquette, Holly Hunter, Isabella Rossellini, Meg Ryan, Michelle Pfeiffer and Daryl Hannah had all been interviewed). 'Uma came to dinner and I knew within minutes that she was Mia.'[17]

From 20 September 1993, they shot in and around Los Angeles, and largely on location: Glendale, North Hollywood, Pasadena, Sun Valley and the Hawthorne Grill for the diner that frames the twisting storylines. In keeping with the backstreet textures of *Reservoir Dogs*, Tarantino intended for *Pulp Fiction* to slip the bonds of its contemporary setting and feel more like the genre-shifting movies of the 1970s, or the pulp fiction of the 1950s. The music, the costumes and the cars (including Vincent prowling around in Tarantino's own 1964 Chevy Malibu convertible) added to the overall effect.

Bruce Willis came as a surprise. They met at a Keitel barbecue. The erstwhile Mr. White, once again fortune's agent, had recently caught up with Willis. The superstar had asked what he had been working on, and Keitel told him about *Reservoir Dogs* and this bright young director who wrote golden dialogue.

Having snared a private audience with the *Pulp Fiction* script, Willis put it to Tarantino straight: 'Whatever you want me to do, I'll do it.'[18] Pay wasn't even a consideration. All the lead actors would work for scale (around $100,000 per person). However, given they got a percentage of the gross, it would prove a very lucrative outing. Willis could sense what Tarantino offered him as an actor – something to say. He considered him as a modern Shakespeare. He had an instinct that he was about to get noticed in a big way.

For Tarantino, Willis had the bruised presence of a 1950s heavy like Aldo Ray or Robert Mitchum, and he immediately thought of him for Butch, the lugubrious boxer attempting to hotfoot from his unfixed fight with his infuriatingly girlish French lover Fabienne (Bender's cherubic ex-girlfriend Marie de Medeiros).

The ensuing pawnshop horrors owe much to pulp author Charles Williford's gifts and Tarantino's disdain for political correctness. In Williford's *Miami Blues* (adapted by George Armitage in 1990) a criminal loses his fingers in a pawnshop break-in. Fleeing, he realizes the fingerprints will identify him and has to go back for them. 'It's a criminal situation which suddenly becomes crazily operatic,' extolled Tarantino, 'but the very absurdity of the event brings it backs to reality.'[19] Which is a fine description of the Tarantino M.O. which revels in the back-and-forth between everyday criminal problems and what he called, 'unexpected dissonances.'[20] Anal rape by rednecks came direct from seeing *Deliverance* aged nine.

Matters of taste are examined by their very absence. From Marvin losing his brains to a careless trigger finger to a katana-sword-wielding Butch, the knee-jerk percussion of violence is designed to make us laugh *and* squirm. As critic Mick LaSalle noted in the *San Francisco Chronicle*, 'With Tarantino we get violence as part of an impish vision of life in which anything can happen – and does.' Death is a punchline.

The absolute apogee of Tarantino's willingness to dare the unthinkable and spin his audience into hysterics centres on a desperate attempt to save a life. Junkie friends had told him that an adrenalin shot could revive a blacked-out OD victim. Tarantino plunges his gangster's moll and her panic-stricken date into a real-life crisis. Mia mistakes Vincent's heroin for coke and ODs, and in one of the most visceral scenes put to film, Vincent must stab a syringe of adrenalin the size of a javelin through her breastplate and into her stopped heart. Her lurch back into consciousness was modelled on seeing a tranquillized tiger come to – it was if the creature had been shot out of a rocket.

Aggrieved to miss out on *Reservoir Dogs*, when the *Pulp Fiction* script arrived Samuel L. Jackson had to read it twice to make sure he 'hadn't been fooling himself'[21]. In a stunning, Biblically charged performance, Jules is the harrumphing, life-altering Abbott to Travolta's sleazy, slippery Costello. 'John and Sam Jackson were so electric together,' thrilled Tarantino, 'that I actually considered making a whole bunch of Vincent and Jules movies.'[22]

From Jackson erupt the film's righteous furies, and his character also spans its redemptive arc. Yet between his expletives there flows a Boy Scout lexicon of 1970s TV jargon that trip straight off the lips of the creator.

This being the Church of Tarantino, the Ezekiel quotation delivered by Jules draws as much on the Sonny Chiba TV series Shadow Warriors' – a Video Archives staple – as 'The Bible. For Tarantino, what was important was that over the course of the film Jules changes and can no longer deliver his pre-hit party piece in the same way. 'For the first time he realizes what it really means. And that's the end of the film.'[23]

**Right:** Vincent (Travolta) and Mia (Thurman) compete in the twist competition at Jack Rabbit Slim's, an image soon to be fixed into movie immortality. While audiences knowingly clocked Travolta's natural dancer's grace, the actor was imagining what it might be like to dance while high on heroin.

As with *Reservoir Dogs*, the possibility of redemption lies at the heart of *Pulp Fiction*: not only in Jules forgoing his hitman life, but Butch choosing to save Marsellus, and Mia's Lazarus-like return from the dead. From a foot massage, to sponging brain matter from automobile upholstery, to rescuing a mob boss from a gimp, *Pulp Fiction* is deeply concerned with the rules that hold this criminal underworld together. It is an unexpectedly ethical film.

As for what's in the case that Jules and Vincent retrieve, Tarantino provides no answer. He stole the idea from the 1955 Mike Hammer-noir *Kiss Me Deadly*, and delighted in the fantastic theories that it spawned (hypothesis numero uno: that it carries Marsellus' soul). Ask actor Roth and he would tell you exactly what he saw: a lamp and a battery.

They had to hurry to get make their coveted slot at the Cannes Film Festival in May 1994, but soaked in European glamour Tarantino was insistent this was the ideal springboard.

If *Reservoir Dogs* had crept up on Cannes by stealth, *Pulp Fiction* arrived like the Fourth of July. A convoy of twenty-five cars spirited them to the Palais. A huge but good-natured crowd spilled back from either side of the red carpet, and as they climbed from their limos a chant of 'Quen-tin! Quent-tin!' was taken up, confirming that it was this raggedy kid from a Manhattan Beach video store, more than his coterie of designer-clad A-list deities, who was the star of the show.

The movie was so recently finished that it hadn't been screened outside of the studio. This was the first time either Jackson or Travolta had seen it. They were in for a rousing evening.

Word broke at the press screening held in advance of the official unveiling

in an unassuming backstreet theatre named the Olympia. *Pulp Fiction* wasn't simply a film it was a seismic cultural event. Tarantino, bursting with confidence and cheek, had made sure he introduced the showing. He asked who there liked *Reservoir Dogs*, and was greeted with a thunderclap of applause. Who liked

*True Romance*, he then enquired of a group of hardened critics in a state of growing hysteria? They applauded all the more. 'Who liked *Remains of the Day*?' he teased. This was met with a smattering of brave claps. 'Get the fuck out of this theater!'[24] he yelled, the goofy grin on the verge of cracking his face wide open.

**Above:** Tarantino was already fully in command of his medium, making films that were emotionally involving while still managing to comment on the idea of movies and play with genre preconceptions.

Thankfully, no one took him at his word, for as Janet Maslin of *The New York Times* said, they were 'about to go down the rabbit hole.' Watching *Pulp Fiction* for the first time was to attend a rock concert in film form; the standard rules of cinematic decorum extinguished by the sheer outrageousness of what was occurring onscreen. As *Entertainment Weekly*'s Owen Gleiberman enthused, 'Watching *Pulp Fiction*, you don't just get engrossed in what's happening on screen. You get intoxicated by it – high on the rediscovery of how pleasurable a movie can be.'

A party-like thrill swept first through the critics and then audiences. Peter Bradshaw in the *Guardian* got poetic on its ass: 'The icy wit, the connoisseur soundtrack, the violence (of which the N-bombs are a part), the extended dialogue riffing, the trance-like unreality ...' The music was indeed integral to the whole effect with Tarantino raiding record stores for a surf guitar vibe: something buoyant and high, pulsating like an over-pumping heartbeat. 'It sounds like rock and roll Spaghetti Western music, and that's how I kind of laid it in.'[25]

Before jetting out of Cannes, Miramax got word it was worth their while hanging around for the award ceremony on the last night of the festival. Tarantino was convinced this meant a token gesture: Best Screenplay, or even a Best Actor award for Travolta. As the ceremony wound on, and those awards were spread among a hatful of fine-tuned international films, Tarantino was bouncing in his seat, losing his cool. Then head of the jury Clint Eastwood opened the envelope and revealed the Palme d'Or: 'Pulp Fiction'. On their way to the stage, a woman jeered (Cannes doesn't hold with award ceremony decorum) and Tarantino turned and flipped her the bird.

Travolta takes credit for persuading Miramax to push the release back from the hurly-burly of summer to a more awards-friendly autumn opening. He wanted to pay back Tarantino for the faith he had shown in him, and one way was to have the film be treated as it should – as a prestige picture. 'This is bigger than even you know,'[26] he insisted prophetically. He might also have had one eye on the possibility of his own Oscar. Nevertheless, Miramax bought into the 'ballsy move'[27], and after another showcase at the New York Film Festival, the film was eventually unleashed on 14 October 1994.

On its opening weekend it made a rousing $9.3 million, and would go on to become the first independent film to break the $100 million mark at the US box office (making $107 million in total in the US). Not for nothing did Miramax dub itself 'the House that Quentin Built'.

**Above:** Lance (Eric Stoltz), Vincent's drug dealer, wearing a Speed Racer T-shirt beneath his permanent bathrobe. The television fodder of Tarantino's youth is referenced through the film — look and listen for everything from 'The Partridge Family' to 'Kung Fu' — and in an early draft the young Butch was going to be watching the 'Speed Racer' cartoon rather than 'Clutch Cargo'.

**Left:** Mia Wallace (Uma Thurman) unwinds at home, prior to her mishap with Vincent's drugs. In a perfectly calibrated (and ironic) choice of song, she is sashaying to the yearning sound of Neil Diamond's 'Girl, You'll be a Woman Soon'.

There was a sour note. When *Pulp Fiction* wrapped, Avary received a letter from Tarantino's lawyer asking him to forfeit his 'written by' credit in exchange for 'story by'. He got straight on the phone to his friend, who came clean: 'I want the credits to end with a title that says, "Written and directed by Quentin Tarantino".'[28] He was willing to admit that the body of The Gold Watch chapter was Avary's work: the absconding boxer, hillbillies and the pawnbroker. But the history of the watch, the writing itself, delivered in a single day's shooting by a sublime Christopher Walken, was entirely his own. At first, Avary resisted. There were things throughout *Pulp Fiction* he felt were his, but hocked up to his gills to get *Killing Zoe* made, he eventually caved in, needing simply to pay his rent. 'But that was the moment a fissure occurred in our relationship.'[29]

**Above:** Jules (Samuel L. Jackson) explains his concept of 'righteous fury' to hold-up merchant Pumpkin (Tim Roth). When he first received the script from Tarantino, Jackson had to read it through twice to make sure it was as good as he initially thought it was. It was.

**Right:** Captain Koons (Christopher Walken) delivers the tale of Butch's father's courage, and of the watch he concealed in an intimate location. Walken's immortal cameo was filmed in a single day. In fact, it was the very last day of filming.

When the film reached the Academy Awards, high on Hollywood's drug of choice in seven Oscar nominations, Tarantino was wise enough to know his chances were slim. Attempts had been made to win over the Academy's notoriously conservative and ageing membership. The director was paraded around like a show-pony, attending every screening and dinner, giving talks, cheerleading and charming as only he could. Miramax spent an estimated $400,000 on their Oscar campaign, and *Pulp Fiction* sauntered off with nearly all the major critics awards. Accepting his Best Screenplay award at the New York Critics Circle dinner (where Robert Redford's *Quiz Show* won Best Picture by a whisker), a beaming Tarantino told the assembled critics he read them all.

Nevertheless, Tarantino's prophecy proved unerring. The Academy conferred a makeweight Best Screenplay Award on the film (picked up by both him and Avary on one of the last occasions they saw one another), but gave the big awards to middlebrow crowd-pleaser *Forrest Gump*. As Weinstein noted philosophically, Tom Hanks could be mayor of Hollywood. Tarantino was still an outsider.

**Right:** The blood- and brain-smeared Vincent (John Travolta) and Jules (Samuel L. Jackson) begin the clean up at Jimmie's place. The black suits were a deliberate nod to the look of *Reservoir Dogs*. Tarantino considered the get-up to be a suit of armour for these guys, but slowly, over the course of the film, their cool exterior will be eroded to reveal a couple of dorks.

He looked tired and irritable on stage as if holding back what he was really thinking. It wasn't his finest monologue as he nervously fumbled his lines. 'This has been a strange year,' he began. 'I can definitely say that.'[30] Behind him Avary squirmed, awaiting his turn.

The following night, Tarantino invited a handful of his old Video Archives buddies to see a rerun of Sergio Leone's *A Fistful of Dollars*. Later they retreated to his suite at the Beverly Hills Hotel to talk and talk like the old times. But that golden statue remained in full view, and they took turns holding it up, knowing this was end of an era.

**Above:** A young Quentin Tarantino in 1994. *Pulp Fiction*, he claimed, embodied his desire to mix things up. The sheer cinematic rush of genre was combined with the realism of actual lives, and things real people talk about.

**Opposite:** Tarantino on the promotional trail in London. If *Reservoir Dogs* had made his reputation, the global success of *Pulp Fiction* turned him into a sensation. As he promoted the film across Europe, he was treated as a bigger star than his cast.

## 'I want the credits to end with a title that says, "Written and directed by Quentin Tarantino".'

*– Quentin Tarantino*

# Once Upon a Time in America

**A complete Quentin Tarantino chronology**

## 1983

**Love Birds in Bondage (short)**
*Director, writer, actor (Boyfriend)*

## 1987

**My Best Friend's Birthday**
*Co-director, co-writer, producer, actor (Clarence Pool)*

## 1988

**Golden Girls
(episode: 'Sophia's Wedding: Part 1)**
*Actor (Elvis impersonator)*

*Quentin Tarantino
as Mr. Brown in
Reservoir Dogs,
1992*

## 1991

**Past Midnight**
*Associate producer,
co-writer (uncredited)*

## 1992

**Reservoir Dogs**
*Director, writer, actor
(Mr. Brown)*

**Eddie Presley**
*Cameo (asylum attendant)*

## 1993

**True Romance**
*Writer*

**Killing Zoe**
*Executive producer*

**Iron Monkey**
*Producer*

christian slater   patricia arquette

STEALING
CHEATING
KILLING

WHO SAYS ROMANCE IS DEAD?

A TONY SCOTT FILM

## TRUE
romance

dennis hopper  val kilmer  gary oldman
brad pitt  christopher walken

Six players on the trail of a half million in cash.
There's only one question...Who's playing who?

**Jackie Brown**
a Quentin Tarantino film

PAM GRIER   SAMUEL L. JACKSON   ROBERT FORSTER   BRIDGET FONDA   MICHAEL KEATON   ROBERT DE NIRO

## 1999

From Dusk Till Dawn 2: Texas Blood Money
*Executive producer*

From Dusk Till Dawn 3: The Hangman's Daughter
*Executive producer*

*Quentin Tarantino with Daryl Hannah on the set of Kill Bill: Volume 1, 2003*

## 1997

**Jackie Brown**
*Director, writer, cameo (answering machine voice)*

## 1998

**God said, 'Ha!'**
*Executive producer, cameo (himself)*

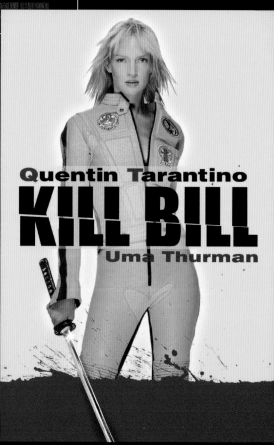

Quentin Tarantino
KILL BILL
Uma Thurman

## 2000

**Little Nicky**
*Actor (Deacon)*

## 2002

**Alias (four episodes)**
*Actor (McKenas Cole)*

## 2003

**Kill Bill: Volume 1**
*Director, writer*

# 1995

- **Destiny Turns on the Radio**
  *Actor (Johnny Destiny)*

- **Crimson Tide**
  *Script doctor (uncredited)*

- **Desperado**
  *Cameo (Pick-up guy)*

- **Leonard Cohen: Dance Me to the End of Love (Short)**
  *Writer, cameo (Groom)*

- **Four Rooms (segment: 'The Man from Hollywood')**
  *Director, writer, executive producer, actor (Chester)*

- **ER (episode 'Motherhood)**
  *Director*

- **All-American Girl (episode: 'Pulp Sitcom')**
  *Actor (Desmond)*

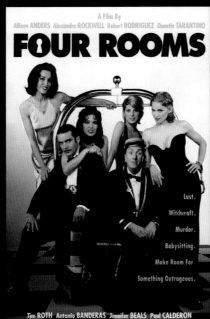

A Film By
Allison ANDERS  Alexandre ROCKWELL  Robert RODRIGUEZ  Quentin TARANTINO

## FOUR ROOMS

Lust.
Witchcraft.
Murder.
Babysitting.
Make Room For
Something Outrageous.

Tim ROTH  Antonio BANDERAS  Jennifer BEALS  Paul CALDERON
Sammi DAVIS  Valeria GOLINO  MADONNA  David PROVAL
Ione SKYE  Lili TAYLOR  Marisa TOMEI  Tamlyn TOMITA

# 1996

- **From Dusk Till Dawn**
  *Writer, executive producer, actor (Richie Gecko)*

- **Girl 6**
  *Cameo (Director #1)*

- **The Rock**
  *Script doctor (uncredited)*

- **Curdled**
  *Producer, co-writer, cameo (Richie Gecko)*

*On the set of Destiny Turns on the Radio, 1995*

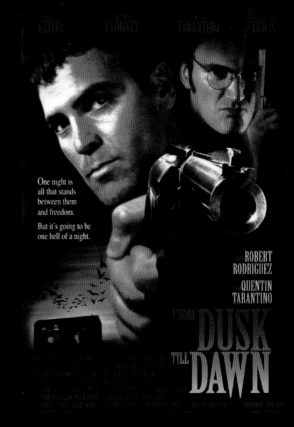

One night is
all that stands
between them
and freedom.

But it's going to be
one hell of a night.

ROBERT
RODRIGUEZ

QUENTIN
TARANTINO

FROM DUSK TILL DAWN

# 1994

- **Natural Born Killers**
  *Story*

- **Sleep With Me**
  *Cameo (Sid)*

- **Pulp Fiction**
  *Director, writer, actor (Jimmie)*

- **It's Pat**
  *Script doctor (uncredited)*

- **Somebody to Love**
  *Cameo (bartender)*

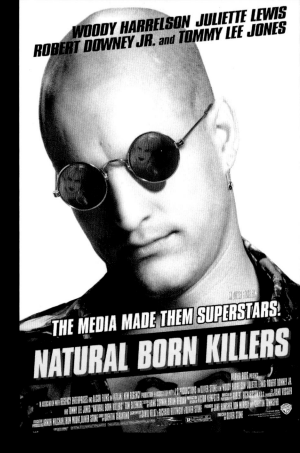

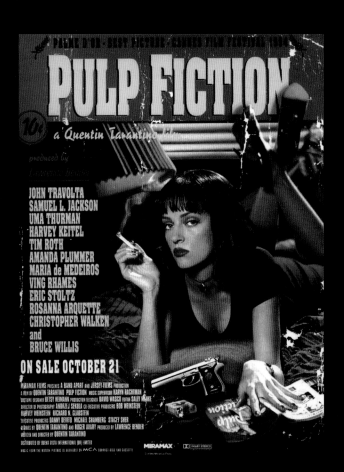

*Quentin Tarantino promoting his film
'Pulp Fiction' at the Bales Hotel in
Kensington, London 1994*

REVENGE IS A DISH BEST
SERVED COLD

**KILL BILL** VOL. 2

THE 5TH FILM BY QUENTIN TARANTINO

MIRAMAX

VOL. 2 IN THEATRES FEBR...

## 2005

**Sin City (scene: Dwight and Jackie Boy in the car)**
*Special guest director*

**CSI: Crime Scene Investigation
(episode: Grave Danger Parts 1 & 2)**
*Director, story*

**Daltry Calhoun**
*Executive producer*

**Hostel**
*Executive producer*

**The Muppets' Wizard of Oz**
*Cameo (Kermit's director)*

## 2006

**Freedom's Fury**
*Executive producer*

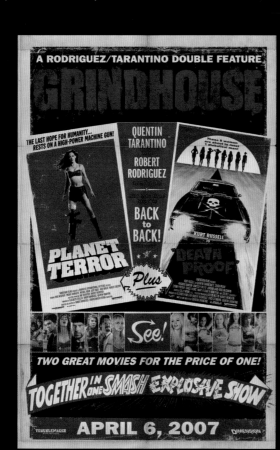

*David Carradine (as Bill) in conversation with Quentin Tarantino on the set of Kill Bill Volume 2*

## 2004

**Kill Bill: Volume 2**
*Director, writer*

**My Name is Modesty: A Modesty Blaise Adventure**
*Executive producer*

A RODRIGUEZ/TARANTINO DOUBLE FEATURE

**GRINDHOUSE**

THE LAST HOPE FOR HUMANITY... RESTS ON A HIGH-POWER MACHINE GUN!

QUENTIN TARANTINO

ROBERT RODRIGUEZ

BACK to BACK!

**PLANET TERROR**

Plus

KURT RUSSELL IS **DEATH PROOF**

See!

TWO GREAT MOVIES FOR THE PRICE OF ONE!

**TOGETHER IN ONE SMASH EXPLOSIVE SHOW**

APRIL 6, 2007

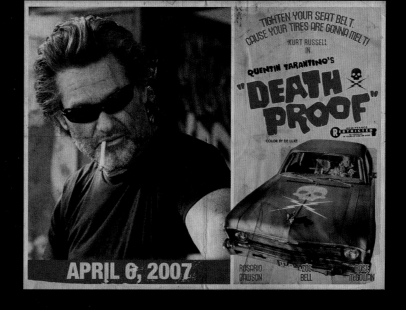

TIGHTEN YOUR SEAT BELT.
CAUSE YOUR TIRES ARE GONNA MELT!

KURT RUSSELL

QUENTIN TARANTINO'S

**"DEATH PROOF"**

COLOR BY DE LUXE

ROSARIO DAWSON  ZOE BELL  ROSE McGOWAN

APRIL 6, 2007

*Quentin Tarantino with Kurt Russell
on the set of Death Proof, 2007*

## 2008

**Sukiyaki Western Django**
*Actor (Piringo)*

**Hell Ride**
*Executive producer*

## 2007

**Grindhouse (segment: 'Planet Terror')**
*Producer, co-writer (uncredited), cameo
(Rapist No. 1 (segment: 'Death Proof')
Director, writer, producer, cameo (Warren)*

**Hostel: Part II**
*Executive producer*

**Death Proof (stand-alone release)**
*Director, writer, producer, cameo (Warren)*

**Planet Terror (stand-alone release)**
*Producer, co-writer (uncredited), cameo
(Rapist No. 1)*

**Diary of the Dead**
*Cameo (voice of newsreader)*

YOU MIGHT FEEL A LITTLE PRICK.

ROBERT RODRIGUEZ'S

**PLANET TERROR**

APRIL 6, 2007

## 2009

**Inglourious Basterds**
*Director, writer, cameo (first scalped Nazi/American Soldier in Pride of a Nation)*

**Softbank (Japanese commercial)**
*Actor (Uncle Tara-chan)*

## 2011

**Kill Bill: The Whole Bloody Affair (DVD release)**
*Director, writer*

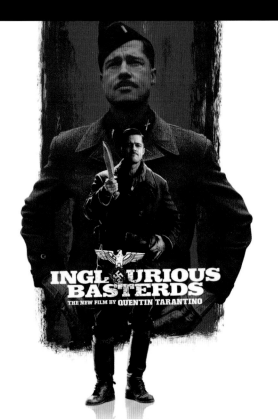

LIFE, LIBERTY AND THE PURSUIT OF VENGEANCE

*Director Quentin Tarantino on the set of Inglourious Basterds, 2009*

## 2012

**Django Unchained**
*Director, writer, actor (The LeQuint Dickey Mining Co. Employee/Robert the Bag Head)*

*Actor and director Quentin Tarantino on the set of Django Unchained, 2012*

## 2014

**She's Funny that Way**
*Cameo (himself)*

## 2015

**The Hateful Eight**
*Director, writer, cameo (narrator)*

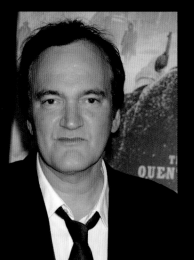

*Quentin Tarantino at the premier of The Hateful Eight, 2015*

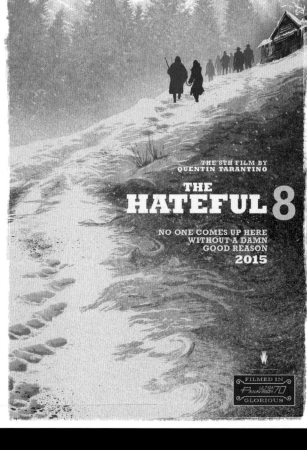

## 2019

**Once Upon a Time in Hollywood**
*Director, producer, writer*

# 'IT JUST KIND OF SNUCK UP ON ME.'

## Four Rooms and Jackie Brown

Quentin Tarantino's name morphed into an adjective sooner than he counted on. Post-*Pulp Fiction*, every third script with a bloody splash of crooks whose plans went awry was suddenly classified as 'Tarantinoesque'. Being overlooked by the Academy – aka the establishment – had only served to reinforce his credibility. Popularity notwithstanding, he remained the brilliant upstart jabbing his finger in the eye of the mainstream.

'I never really understood what Tarantinoesque means,'[1] he groaned. He didn't find the term particularly flattering, it was too specific: the suits, the 'hipper than thou'[2] dialogue and references to old TV shows. He began to rail against the story of the geek that made good. The film lover was just one facet of his personality, he insisted, 'one of the heads of the dragon.'[3] He wanted to impress upon fans and critics that there was more to his work, a desire that would lead him back to the inspiration of Elmore Leonard and *Jackie Brown*.

First though, came the backlash. It was how the universe worked. No-one could be declared the new Orson Welles, the chosen one who would straddle the worlds of the arthouse and commercial filmmaking, without some karmic payback. The skill was to ride it out, and not go the way of Welles: exiled from the magic kingdom, squandering your own talent. It centred on the strange case of *Four Rooms*.

A kinship had endured between the bright, young things who had made such a noise at Sundance in 1992: Tarantino, Alexandre Rockwell (*In the Soup*), Allison Anders (*Gas Food Lodging*), Richard Linklater (*Dazed and Confused*) and Robert Rodriguez (*El Mariachi*). They were the 'class of 92', the fast-talking vanguard of a new indie scene. They started to think of themselves as the equivalent of the Movie Brats of the 1970s, or the French New Wave. Whenever they met, they began to talk of an anthology film they would make together to commemorate the moment, each contributing in their own hip style. Somewhere along the line it got serious, although *Five Rooms* would be downscaled to *Four* when Linklater dropped out.

**Above:** Quentin Tarantino mid-joke in his extended cameo in pal Robert Rodriguez's *Desperado*. With his newfound celebrity, Tarantino enjoyed feeding the wannabe actor inside of him, even if the critical reception was decidedly mixed.

Six players on the trail of a half million in cash.
There's only one question...Who's playing who?

**Jackie Brown.**

This Christmas, Santa's got a brand new bag.

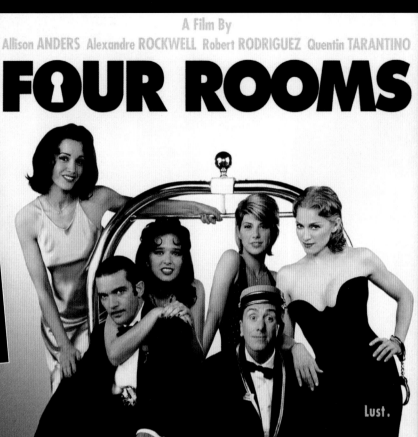

A Film By

Allison ANDERS  Alexandre ROCKWELL  Robert RODRIGUEZ  Quentin TARANTINO

# FOUR ROOMS

Lust.

Witchcraft.

Murder.

Babysitting.

Make Room For

Something Outrageous.

Tim ROTH  Antonio BANDERAS  Jennifer BEALS  Paul CALDERON
Sammi DAVIS  Valeria GOLINO  MADONNA  David PROVAL
Ione SKYE  Lili TAYLOR  Marisa TOMEI  Tamlyn TOMITA

**Above:** The poster for *Jackie Brown* played up its upmarket ensemble. Choosing to directly adapt Elmore Leonard's *Rum Punch* had come as a surprise, not least to Tarantino himself, but having picked up the rights to the book he found he couldn't let it go.

**Right:** The poster for ill-fated portmanteau movie *Four Rooms*. While conceived with the best intentions, the group effort from the stars of Sundance 1992 was poorly thought out and rushed into production, proving that native talent wasn't enough. Tarantino doesn't consider his segment among his 'official' films.

**Right:** *Four Rooms* quartet of friends and directors, from the left: Robert Rodriguez, Allison Anders, Alexandre Rockwell and Quentin Tarantino, with producer Lawrence Bender behind the sofa. The film would prove a severe testing ground for the durability of their friendship.

If *Pulp Fiction* jazzily syncopated the anthology concept, *Four Rooms* played it straight: each director would tell a story apiece, each set in a different room of a swish Hollywood hotel. Effectively each of them would only be making a short, linked by the involvement of the bellhop Ted.' The weight of the world wouldn't be riding on it,'[4] noted Tarantino.

Anders, determined to use a female ensemble, lit upon a coven of modern-day witches in need of a sample of Ted's sperm to conclude their spell. They even included Madonna in their number. Amusingly, now the talk of the town, Tarantino had met the queen of pop at her office in New York. She presented him with a copy of her new album, *Erotica*, on which she had written about the true meaning of 'Like a Virgin': 'To Quentin – it's about love, not dick.'[5]

Rockwell classified his entry as a weird psychodrama, inspired by daytime soaps (and secretly a story he once heard about Sean Penn and Madonna). Heading to the wrong room Ted becomes embroiled in the S&M antics of a husband and wife, played by Rockwell's real wife Jennifer Beals (tied to a chair) and David Proval (waving a gun).

Rodriguez cut against the adult grain with a family comedy. As rich couple Antonio Banderas and Tamlyn Tomita head out on the town, they bribe Ted into keeping an eye on what turn out to be their outrageously badly behaved children. Roger Ebert in the *Chicago Sun-Times* claimed this frenetic episode was the reason to see the film: 'This is slapstick on a grand scale, acted and edited with perfect comic timing.'

Tarantino's 'room' – the last and longest – possessed an aura of self-parody. After a string of bad reviews for his recent cameos in *Sleep With Me*, *Destiny Turns on the Radio* and *Desperado*, he channelled his frustrations into *Four Rooms*. Up in the penthouse, he stars as Chester Rush, a director fresh off a massive debut. 'You can see the vulnerability in it,'[6] said Rockwell. Chester entices Ted to join in their New Year's revelry. Inspired by an old Peter Lorre-Steve McQueen episode of 'Alfred Hitchcock Presents' entitled *Man from the South* (which he had never seen), Chester and his cronies bet a man's little finger on the catch of a cigarette lighter.

'[Chester] ended up shouldering some of my baggage as a celebrity,' remarked Tarantino. 'The media is so fucking sick of me'[7]. He was barely two films into his career and three biographies had been published, running a spectrum from high praise to open criticism. Playing Chester was supposed to be an exorcism.

The four directors assembled for a night in the Chateau Marmont, the celebrated hotel masquerading as a Bavarian castle on Sunset Boulevard and prototype for their Hotel Mon Signor. They would map out their stories, and the framing mechanism in which Ted is shown the ropes. 'It was like a big pyjama party,' said Rockwell, recalling that they got take-out and brought videos. 'It was like Quentin's fantasy night.'[8]

Problems arose swiftly. The part of Ted the bellhop was written to chime with Steven Buscemi's nervous tics, confident that he would rise to the challenge. But he turned them down, worried the part was too close to the bellhop he played in the Coens' *Barton Fink* (which was partly the point),

**Above:** The coven of witches from Anders' heavily compromised segment of *Four Rooms, The Missing Ingredient*. From the left: Madonna, Sammi Davis, Valeria Golino, Lili Taylor and Ione Skye. Anders was delighted at how readily Madonna was willing to send up her own image.

freaked out, thought Rockwell, by the idea of responding to four different directors.

So they turned to Tim Roth, who was intrigued by the challenge of physical comedy and maintaining a uniform (indeed uniformed) character between four different directors.

Entering production there was the inescapable feeling that they were winging it. As Rodriguez admitted, 'We didn't realize what we were making until it was done.'[9] Tarantino and producer Lawrence Bender had maintained it had to be done cheaply. Anthology films were always a risk. Hence *Four Rooms* cost Miramax only $4 million, but the lack of investment is exposed in the thin sets and lack of variety.

Friendships were sorely tested.

Weeks before they were due to begin production, Tarantino had almost backed out. He had called Anders, as she put it,

'totally overstressed.'[10] Anders appealed to his loyalty, and the fact that the point of no return was now miles behind them. When the first cut came in at two and a half hours, Miramax began to stress. This was supposed to be a comedy. Given Rodriguez's rat-a-tat-tat section was an already economical 24 minutes, and Miramax weren't about to ask Tarantino to trim his characteristic languorous takes, it fell to Anders and Rockwell to prune their entries. Any sense of personality or tension was lost from the opening two stories and the entire edifice felt hopelessly lopsided.

Rodriguez's few bright moments aside, it was an indulgent mess, made on a whim, poorly thought out, and rushed into cinemas in a fit of hubris (however well-meaning). The styles jar, the jokes are flat and Roth, working his socks off, falls far short of the Jerry Lewis-Peter Sellers-style

mugging required. There are hints of the Tarantino groove in the fourth room, but the characters, usually his forte, remain shapelessly first base and horribly smug.

Not unexpectedly, the reviews were damning. Many critics were appalled at the laziness and conceit on show. Owen Gleiberman in *Entertainment Weekly* soured to 'a general atmosphere of cultivated obnoxiousness.' 'The less said about this career denting fiasco the better,' spat Janet Maslin in *The New York Times*, shocked to be so let down by the creative force she had championed.

**Above:** The chaotic family of Robert Rodriguez's slapstick-styled segment *The Misbehavers*, clockwise from top left: Tamlyn Tomita, Antonio Banderas, Danny Verduzco and Lana McKissack. Indicative of the hurried nature of the project, Rodriguez shot his story one week after completing *Desperado*.

The New York Film Festival rejected it outright. And the audience wasn't buying either. The box office returns were negligible, with $4.2 million in the US. It was his first true taste of failure, and no-one in the end was as exposed as Tarantino. *Four Rooms* was almost a self-fulfilling prophecy – a personal invitation to the backlash. His joke about being overexposed only proved how overexposed he was. And now that nemesis had arrived. As the media delighted to put him in his place, Tarantino decided to sit it out. He was going to take a year off.

'Life's just too short to do movie after movie after movie,' he mused. 'It's like getting married to get married. I wanna be in love and say, "This is the woman".'[11]

Right about then, he admitted, he never wanted to make another movie. It was a period of reappraisal and recuperation. What's more, he was naturally lazy, he would often tell journalists. Unless ensnared by the drug-like surge of a movie, he would happily drift along.

**Above:** Jennifer Beals, David Proval and Tim Roth in Alexandre Rockwell's segment *The Wrong Man*. Beals, Rockwell's real-life wife, was the only actor apart from Tim Roth to appear in more than one story. She also featured in Tarantino's offering *The Man From Hollywood*.

**Above:** The cast of Quentin Tarantino's segment, *The Man From Hollywood*, from left: an uncredited Bruce Willis, Tarantino, Paul Calderón and Jennifer Beals. Despite the brevity of the short story format, Tarantino still managed to work in his trademark long takes and 193 uses of the word 'fuck'.

**Opposite:** Bellhop Ted (Tim Roth) is shocked by the entreaties of Tarantino's director Chester. Tarantino was aiming to send up his own image with this tale of a hotshot director, with only one film to his name, already drunk on the Hollywood lifestyle.

'Friendships were sorely tested. "We didn't realize what we were making until it was done." '

– Robert Rodriguez

Throughout his career, Tarantino would periodically go off the grid, unplugging the phone and welcoming the embrace of silence. Not that he had exactly reverted to his old scruffy life, there was still a standing dinner invitation from Arnold Schwarzenegger and he 'wanted to hang out with Warren Beatty some more'.[12]

Fame was a tricky deal. When he attended a *Get Shorty* screening – a terrific Elmore Leonard adaptation over which John Travolta had dithered until Tarantino urged him to stop fooling around – he wanted to get out of the VIP seats and sit up close to the screen with the kids. He soon began to be harassed for an autograph. 'Not when I'm in a movie man,' he snapped. 'I'm here to see a movie like you and you got to respect that, you know?'[13]

Partly of his own making, Tarantino wasn't famous like a director; he was as recognizable as a movie star.

The break was also a chance to cook up the second phase of his career. He needed to leave behind the world of crime, not wanting, as he said, to be 'the gun guy'[14] for evermore. 'I want to do a Western,'[15] he admitted. Soon enough, Tarantino's sabbatical was hectic with everything but directing.

There were more positive, if equally uneconomical, expansions of the Tarantino brand. He persuaded Miramax to allow him to launch his own label, Rolling Thunder (named after a William Devane revenge flick), that would release those Eastern cinema and exploitation movies that would otherwise go straight to video (if they were lucky). As a favour, he worked, uncredited, sprucing up the script on Tony Scott's *Crimson Tide*. 'I'm very proud of what I did,'[16] he said of his script doctoring of the submarine epic. Except for a couple of scenes, the first 45 minutes of the film, 'Every time someone opens their mouth, it's me.'[17] He was growing ticked off with the way it was inferred that all he had done was sprinkle a few mentions of the Silver Surfer and *Star Trek* about the deck.

There are stories too that Tarantino applied some vernacular varnish to Michael Bay's actioner *The Rock*, while completists, who strive to consume ever syllable of Tarantino's making, also cite his undetectable input into one-joke comedy *It's Pat*, starring his good friend Julia Sweeney from 'Saturday Night Live'. He also had a ball directing the 'ER' episode *Motherhood*. It was one of their bloodiest storylines, featuring a female gang fight in the hospital, where one girl slices the ear off another.

Meanwhile, he traded in his West Hollywood apartment for a mansion in the Hollywood Hills overlooking the Universal lot. Soon dubbed The Castle, he filled its halls with memorabilia, a shrine to his love of movies, and spent a year designing and building his own fifty-seat home cinema, with a red plush sofa out front reserved just for him.

Most of all, however, he was generating a fresh store of creative energy, rediscovering his filmmaking mojo in a most unexpected place – officially adapting someone else's work. Less unexpectedly, that source turned out to be the crime novelist Elmore Leonard. For the time being, he would still be the 'gun guy'. Well, sorta.

To some degree, all of Tarantino's work to date had been unofficially adapting Leonard's rap sheet of novels (he was, after all, a master of pulp fiction). Leonard was the first novelist who really spoke to him. 'His style dictated my style to some degree,'[18] Tarantino openly admitted. Leonard's loose, comic plots skirt the edges of the real world.

While in pre-production on *Pulp Fiction*, Tarantino had read the galley proofs of the latest Leonard novel, entitled *Rum Punch* – which would eventually become *Jackie Brown*. 'I just kind of saw the movie,'[19] he said, and was stirred enough to look into the rights, but Leonard's camp required he confirm it as his next film. With no certainty of where his head would be after *Pulp Fiction*, he let it go.

With his stock still running high at Miramax, when the rights to three of Leonard's novels later became available they picked up *Freaky Deaky*, *Killshot* and, as fate would have it, *Rum Punch* as a gift for their prize asset. His first thought was to produce a version of *Rum Punch*, and he had a director in mind. But reading it again, he found that movie was still lurking in his head. 'It just kind of snuck up on me,'[20] he admitted.

He would re-embrace the milieu of *Pulp Fiction*, but make a film in striking contrast to its cool playfulness. His adaptation, now retitled *Jackie Brown*, would run chronologically, A to B to C. To Tarantino's zigzagging sensibility this was a radical subversion of the norm. 'I wasn't trying to top *Pulp Fiction* with *Jackie Brown*, I wanted to go underneath it and make a more modest character study movie.'[21] If his previous film had been an opera, this was a chamber piece. He already had a readymade subgenre for what he had in mind: this was a 'hang out'

movie. 'I made *Jackie Brown* like the way I always felt about [Howard Hawks'] *Rio Bravo*, which is a movie I can watch every couple of years.'[22] Once you get the storyline out of the way, you simply enjoy 'hanging out' with the characters.

A very strange word started being bandied around in relation to the new film. Tarantino was trying out 'maturity' for size. The new film would still touch on themes present in his previous work – obligation, responsibility and the façade of honour (those rules and regulations of his criminal hinterland) – but the pace and mood remained chilled, with the characters given even more room to breathe.

'Quentin's got rid of all that star stuff he was so fond of,' elaborated Samuel L. Jackson, who would feature as the scheming Ordell Robbie. 'When he started writing scripts it was because he wanted to be a movie star like a lot of people do. Then when he became Quentin Tarantino – the star moviemaker, he rode that … He bought into it for a while, had some fun with it, and now he's been burned. He's learned from it. He's grown.'[23]

While faithful to the book, Tarantino knew nothing of its Miami setting. So he transplanted the story to the familiar backwaters of Los Angeles (and changed the name). It was something he could offer Leonard, the grain of his own world.

They shot across the summer of 1997 in and around the South Bay area, Tarantino's old stomping ground. The telescoped captions – City of Carson; City of Hawthorne – added to the patchwork texture of a real city; a contemporary LA as beat-up as the characters. The film may be an adaptation, but it wears familiar clothing. The finale, involving a three-way bag switch and three dead bodies, takes place among the regular bustle of shoppers at the Del Amo Mall, a frequent hang out from Tarantino's idler days.

Far less self-consciously shot than *Pulp Fiction*, if anything the direction is even more assured than its showier predecessors. The only time Tarantino messes with time is when seeing the final con from a tangle of viewpoints, switching songs with each. There are occasional flares of invention and homage – split screens, deep focus, that sly omission of master shots to conceal characters outside of the frame – but overall he pursued a more fluid, improvisational style, letting his actors drive the scene.

The casting was if anything more crucial than before. Going against Hollywood thinking, he needed older lives at the centre of his film. Actors who could embody something careworn and bruised; the two leads weren't career criminals, but working joes whose lives intersect with low-level crooks and the cynical machinations of the FBI. There was next to none of those detours into pop culture; this was as real as he would ever get. The script, which Leonard proclaimed masterful, contained about half Tarantino and half the author's dialogue, but the seam was impossible to detect.

Tarantino wanted 'lived in', not 'movie characters'[24], yet when it came to the book's beleaguered protagonist Jackie Burke, the air-stewardess plying a low-level smuggling racket on the side whom he would smooth

out into Jackie Brown, his first thought was a long-limbed starlet of the blaxploitation craze of the 1970s.

Pam Grier had got a name check in *Reservoir Dogs*. In Video Archives the blaxploitation collection was Tarantino's personal domain. He would regularly insist a customer rethink their choice in favour of *Foxy Brown*, *Coffy* or *Scream Blacula Scream*. Grier had screen-tested for the roles of Mia and Jody in *Pulp Fiction*. She didn't fit then, but he promised he would return. When she came in to talk about *Jackie Brown*, there were posters on his office wall from her belt of 1970s B-movies. She wondered if that was specifically for her benefit? No, he had been meaning to take them down for her benefit.

He also knew that as Grier had got older, she had stretched into theatre acting. She was capable of 'truly great character work.'[25]

Jackie had been written as caucasian, but making her black would 'give her more moral depth.'[26] Survival would be more of an instinct. She was also imbued with the single-mindedness and determination Tarantino had seen in his mother; a woman, he said, who had pulled herself 'up by her bootstraps.'[27] Unsurprisingly then, it is Connie's favourite of his movies.

Grier went hard at the role, pasting a 12-foot log of the script to her hotel room wall, telling her where Jackie was, inside, as the plot swerved around. They would shoot wildly out of sequence, but she maintained a tender but resolute portrayal of a woman scurrying for a second chance.

The film's glorious opening sequence (arguably the best of Tarantino's career) is such a statement of intent. Without a single word, in a lingering tracking shot, we watch Grier's Jackie stroll sexily through LAX airport to the silken groove of Bobby Womack's 'Across 110th Street'. If propulsive surf music was the vibe for *Pulp Fiction*, then Tarantino explained, 'Old-school soul is the rhythm and feel this film takes place to.'[28] The scene was an in-joke, not only at the expense of the director's prolix habits, but also of Grier's hot-chick past. So many of those blaxploitation classics began with Grier simply walking. So Tarantino thought, 'Okay, I will make me the greatest Pam Grier opening sequence of all time.'[29]

This was Foxy Brown twenty years on, still sexy and indomitable. Only towards the end of the unbroken shot, she starts to dash, suddenly harried and urgent, and we realize this is a woman late for work. It's a gorgeously subtle change: the smooth transformation from an expectation into the reality. From Foxy Brown into Jackie Brown, a woman with worries.

'Some baggage,' noted Tarantino, 'can be very good.'[30]

When it came to Max Cherry, the job-sore bail bondsman looking for a way out, Tarantino drew up a wish list that included Paul Newman, 1970s hard man John Saxon and Gene Hackman, but Robert Forster had no baggage. Rather than the aura of the past with which Grier would enrich Jackie, Tarantino wanted Max to be a relatively blank presence – an ordinary guy, his better days behind him. Hackman would crowd out the movie with his authority. Forster was harder to place.

Tarantino knew him well, of course, from the likes of *Medium Cool*, *Reflections in a Golden Eye* and the TV series 'Banyon', which only lasted a season. He was another actor whose shine had dulled, and was making ends meet doing motivational speeches. That seen-and–fucking-done-it-all quality spoke volumes, extolled Tarantino, 'Robert Forster's face is backstory.'[31] All the successes, and the heartbreaks, it was right there.

Forster also had prior with Tarantino. He had been up for the Lawrence Tierney role in *Reservoir Dogs*, but it hadn't worked out. Tarantino promised to make good on it. Eighteen months before *Jackie Brown* they had bumped into one other in Forster's regular breakfast diner. Tarantino told him to read *Rum Punch*, because he was currently adapting it. Five months later,

Forster strolled back into the diner to find Tarantino sitting in his favourite spot, a script on the table in front of him. There was something sweet, the director reflected, 'in giving him another day in court, seeing what a good actor he is.'[32] He wondered how many more Griers and Forsters were out there.

Nothing in Tarantino's work had given the slightest hint that he was capable of the gentle gravity of Jackie and Max hesitantly falling for one another. This was true romance. He described them as 'people with decisions to make,'[33] as if they were operating outside of his control. As if nothing in the film was predetermined by the fixtures of plot. This was life.

Continuing a flourishing partnership, he could picture Ordell Robbie in the capable hands of Samuel L. Jackson. Bridget Fonda was Ordell's nagging beachbum girlfriend Melanie, and in a surprisingly comic turn Robert De Niro plays slovenly ex-con Louis. He and Tarantino had met at the Munich Film Festival, and talked about nothing but movies. When Lawrence Bender passed on the script, De Niro saw the ironic value in Louis. Communicating largely through a medley of grunts and shrugs, he was the exact opposite of what we would have expected of the great De Niro stepping into Tarantino's world.

Indeed, the film greatly confounded expectations. It was subtle and slow-moving, and the body count was down to a feeble four victims. Still, Tarantino would be attacked for his unwillingness to shy away from the profane street slang of his characters. Whereas that trigger word 'nigger' was voiced twenty-eight times in *Pulp Fiction*, it was casually thrown in ten more times in *Jackie Brown* – usually out of the mouth of Jackson's Ordell. Director Spike

Lee, supposedly a friend, was vociferous in his condemnation of *Jackie Brown*'s appropriation of black language.

Tarantino remained unrepentant. He was drawing on the street culture of his youth. It was there too in the blaxploitation films he was referencing. Jackson, hastening to his director's defence, was determined this was simply storytelling. If that's the story you have inside of you, so be it. 'Ordell talks the way Ordell talks,' he fumed. 'That is who he is.'[34]

*Jackie Brown* was 'Tarantino's most complex and revelatory examination of unfulfilled love.' Nevertheless, the film was hardly a sensation, making $40 million in the US, which felt like a flop, even if on a modest budget of $12 million it did make money. Only in hindsight has it become one of his most significant films: a mark of something emotionally deeper than the genre-shattering thrill of his first releases.

Indeed, Tarantino made it clear, in the few interviews he agreed to, that *Jackie Brown* didn't dwell within his shared universe. He was relaxing in Leonard's universe. He even struck a pact with Steven Soderbergh that Michael Keaton would appear again as the neurotic FBI agent Ray Nicolette in Soderbergh's adaption of Leonard's *Out of Sight*. That said, Jackie drives not just a similar Honda Civic, but *the* battered Honda Civic Butch has in *Pulp Fiction*, itself a tribute to the rattletrap Honda that was Tarantino's first car.

Introducing his film at London's National Film Theatre, Tarantino declared that he saw *Jackie Brown* as a black film made for a black audience: 'Don't let the pigmentation fool ya, it's a state of mind.'

Released on Christmas Day 1997, it had been three years since *Pulp Fiction*. The fervour had dimmed, and *Jackie Brown* served notice that Tarantino was still doing his own thing. He had resisted Miramax's urges to cut thirty minutes from its languid 154 minutes running time. He also resisted the calls for interviews (he was sick of listening to himself), and harkening to a different urge hid himself inside the character of the psycho in a revival of *Wait Until Dark* on Broadway alongside Marisa Tomei (who had a cameo in *Four Rooms*). Which led to another bruising encounter with the critics.

*Jackie Brown*, meanwhile, was largely admired. 'Most striking is the film's gallantry and sweetness,' wrote David Ansen in *Newsweek*. *Slant*'s Glenn Heath Jr. saw that

**Left:** Jackie Brown (Pam Grier) consults with FBI agent Ray Nicolette (Michael Keaton). Much as he had with John Travolta in *Pulp Fiction*, Tarantino wanted to infuse the part of Jackie with Grier's past as a blaxploitation star. A big fan, Tarantino had always wanted to direct her in something.

**Below:** Louis (Robert De Niro) makes his feeling known to the irksome Melanie (Bridget Fonda). Elmore Leonard, who served as executive producer, considered the film to be the best adaption of his work. Asked for his opinion, he simply replied, 'That was my novel.'

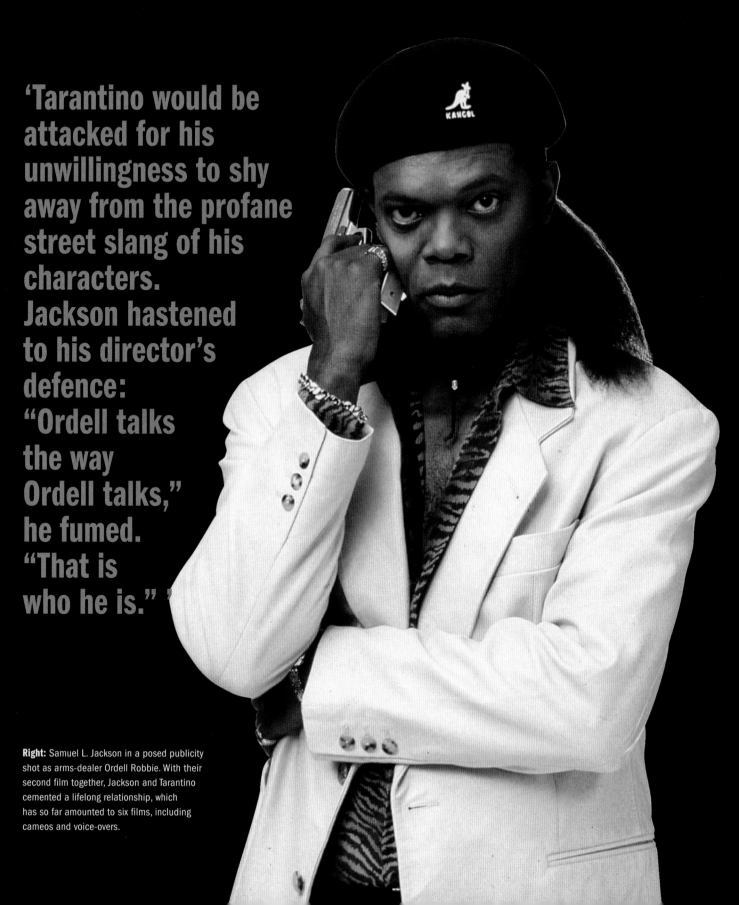

'Tarantino would be attacked for his unwillingness to shy away from the profane street slang of his characters. Jackson hastened to his director's defence: "Ordell talks the way Ordell talks," he fumed. "That is who he is." '

**Right:** Samuel L. Jackson in a posed publicity shot as arms-dealer Ordell Robbie. With their second film together, Jackson and Tarantino cemented a lifelong relationship, which has so far amounted to six films, including cameos and voice-overs.

# 'I DON'T REALLY CONSIDER MYSELF AN AMERICAN FILMMAKER...'

## Kill Bill: Volumes 1 and 2

Six years passed without a new film by Quentin Tarantino. With them went the down-and-dirty picture scene of which he had been crown prince. In his absence, independent filmmaking drew back into itself, back to the prim Sundance model filled with manners and anguish. Back to the teacups and pursed lips of the Merchant-Ivory school, the relationship movies he derided.

Meanwhile, Tarantino's peers had either gone mainstream, like Robert Rodriguez, or gone missing. It was as if *Jackie Brown* had been a brief interruption of what was now a self-imposed exile. Had that all-consuming passion left him?

The truth was Tarantino could afford to wait until he was good and ready. He was rediscovering the fecund spirit he had before *Reservoir Dogs*, only now he didn't need to work. As he put it, 'I get to live the life of an artist.'[1]

He was readying a new store of material, the next chapter in his career, and this was just one of those classic longueurs before the thrills kick in. When he wasn't hanging out, he was watching movies, filling his head with images, and writing, still with two felt-tip pens, one red, one black – just like The Bride will use for her hit list.

For his comeback, he planned to make the loudest, craziest, most reverential – and least realistic – film possible. The Fourth Film by Quentin Tarantino, as it was flamboyantly billed, would double down on what we had come to know as Tarantinoesque. In short, he was about to try his hand at an action movie. Not in any mainstream Hollywood sense, but as a tribute to the myriad of martial arts films that sprang out of Japan, Korea and China. Films like the Sonny Chiba double-bill that Clarence savours in a rundown cinema at the beginning of *True Romance*. It would be blood-soaked like never before and bound around the globe.

Tarantino saw it as a natural progression. 'I don't really consider myself an American filmmaker like, say, Ron Howard might be considered an American filmmaker.'[2]

**Above:** Quentin Tarantino with Daryl Hannah as the one-eyed assassin Elle Driver. The Deadly Viper Assassination Squad was inspired by the fake television pilot, 'Fox Force Five', that Tarantino created for Mia Wallace in *Pulp Fiction*.

Quentin Tarantino

**KILL BILL**

Uma Thurman

All this ran counter to the initial perception of him as a markedly American filmmaker, with Los Angeles his canvas. This was to be a return and a reinvention. He went on, 'If I'm going to do something that begs to be done in the vein of a Japanese Yakuza movie, or Hong Kong Triad movie, I'm gonna do it like that.'[3] *Kill Bill* was going to be the kind of film the characters in other Tarantino films talked about.

Its inception can be traced to some barroom banter between the director and Uma Thurman in the early days of *Pulp Fiction*. Over beers they dreamed up an elaborate tale of revenge set initially against a gangster milieu and centred on the deadliest assassin in the world. Over the next few weeks, still shooting *Pulp Fiction* by day, they would elaborate on their schemes for this retired killer, left for dead, betrayed by her former squad, who returns to pick them off one-by-one.

Thurman suggested that in the opening scene, with the protagonist shot in the head, the camera pulls back to reveal chillingly that she is wearing a wedding dress. And so she became The Bride (the character will be credited to 'Q & U').

It was Tarantino, naturally, who decided to marry The Bride's righteous mission to the martial arts genre. A path of destruction that would gradually lead, by elaborately choreographed steps, towards her former mentor – and, as we shall learn, lover – head of the Deadly Viper Assassination Squad, the elusive Bill. The title was almost inevitable.

The film would be divided into a typically complex and madly intermingled set of chapters, yet somehow always moving headlong towards its destiny.

**THIS OCTOBER, GO FOR THE KILL**

UMA IS THE BRIDE
LUCY IS COTTONMOUTH!
MICHAEL IS SIDEWINDER
VIVICA IS COPPERHEAD
GORDON IS CRAZY 88
CHIAKI IS GO GO

THE 4TH FILM BY QUENTIN TARANTINO

**KILL BILL**

This page and opposite: Some of the many iterations of the poster for both volumes of *Kill Bill* from around the world. Interestingly, and erroneously, the *Kill Bill Vol. 2* poster classifies it as the fifth film by Quentin Tarantino when they should be considered together as the fourth.

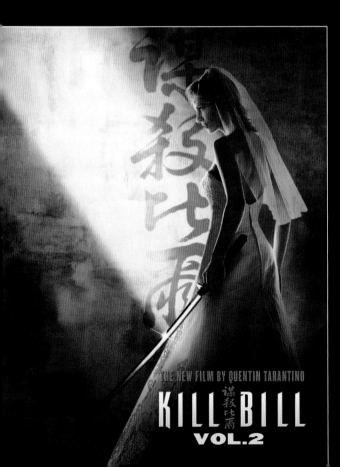

THE NEW FILM BY QUENTIN TARANTINO

**KILL BILL**
**VOL.2**

REVENGE IS A DISH BEST SERVED COLD

VOL. 2

**KILL BILL**

THE 5TH FILM BY QUENTIN TARANTINO

Tarantino had dashed down their preliminary ideas on a few pages before tossing them into a drawer to be forgotten. Time passed. *Pulp Fiction* and *Jackie Brown* made their contrasting impacts. Finally, he ran into Thurman at an industry party, and she reminded him of the plan they had hatched for lady vengeance. That was when inspiration struck like a cobra bite. Tarantino dug out those old pages and began to write … What a way, he thought, to make a comeback … To almost overdose on movieness.

The Bride, who has spent four years in a coma as the film revs up, was written entirely for Thurman. She was as essential to the film as Harvey Keitel was to *Reservoir Dogs*. She was, in all fairness, the co-author. So when Thurman became pregnant, Tarantino was willing to delay the shoot another year, and wait out the birth of her son Roan. He put it to Miramax in grand terms. 'If Josef von Sternberg is getting ready to make *Morocco* and Marlene Dietrich gets pregnant, he waits.'[4] Which also gives an extra edge to Thurman's portrayal of The Bride, who will discover the daughter she thinks miscarried is alive and living with Bill.

As with all his main characters, The Bride was also an avatar of Tarantino. 'I started taking on little feminine tendencies during the writing process,'[5] he confessed. He found it refreshing. Here, at last, truly, was his girl with a gun (okay, sword). She also served as a metaphor for Tarantino, awakening from his coma, and meting out his revenge on all those who had doubted him.

*Kill Bill* sits outside of the Tarantino universe shared by *Reservoir Dogs* and *Pulp Fiction*, which are within reach of the real world. This is what he defines as his 'movie-movie universe'[6] completely detached from reality (and shared by *From*

*Dusk Till Dawn*, as marked by the presence of Michael Parks' Sheriff McGraw, who also features in *Grindhouse*). In the movie-movie universe the heroine can turn to the camera, while piloting a VW camper van against an apocalyptic desert skyline, and report that thus far we can attribute her actions to a 'rip-roaring rampage of revenge.'[7] It celebrated its own artifice.

Nevertheless, contrary to the idea of Tarantino as an ironic filmmaker,

celebrating obscure pop cultural doodads and riffing on forgotten movies, he is a genuine enthusiast. His is not some kind of clever-clever detachment. He claims not to know what irony really means; all his fakery is for real. He is subverting genre, but never selling it out. This is an authentic version of how he processes the world, how he thinks through a stream of conscious flicker-book of all the hundreds and thousands of movies he has taken in.

**Above:** The Deadly Viper Squad at the scene of their betrayal. From the left: Californian Mountain Snake (Elle Driver, played by Daryl Hannah), Copperhead (Vernita Green, played by Vivica A. Fox), Sidewinder (Budd, played by Michael Madsen), and Cottonmouth (O-Ren Ishii, played by Lucy Liu).

**Opposite:** Lucy Lui as O-Ren Ishii at the House of Blue Leaves. If you follow the film's twisted chronology, O-Ren is actually the first of The Bride's victims, but the titanic battle with the Yakuza boss' army of bodyguards was conceived as the perfect culmination of the first Volume.

*Kill Bill* was shock therapy – a Tarantino fest in film form. He literally incorporated other films into the fabric of his story, rather than having his characters discuss them. 'There was an aspect of The Bride not just fighting through her death list, she was fighting through the whole history of exploitation cinema, with every character on that list representing a different genre.'[8]

The scattered members of the disbanded Deadly Vipers were like the 'flip side'[9] of the crime fighting 'Fox Force Five', the TV pilot mentioned in *Pulp Fiction* that featured Thurman's Mia Wallace. Each is codenamed for a snake, each relocated across the planet, and each with their own personality and concomitant fighting style. They were to be played by Daryl Hannah, Lucy Liu, Vivica A. Fox and Michael Madsen.

Good-luck charm Samuel L. Jackson has a cameo as Rufus, the organ player at the fateful chapel (he also provides narration for a couple of scenes).

'It crosses every genre,'[10] laughed Tarantino insanely. This was his kung-fu movie, his samurai movie, his badass chick epic, another Spaghetti Western, his Grindhouse picture and his comic-book movie. It was as if a tornado had torn through Video Archives scattering tapes in all directions. There was even an anime sequence, to tell the Yakuza-themed backstory of Liu's seductive O-Ren Ishii. Given he could manage no more than stick figures, Tarantino wrote a long, elaborate list of the shots that he wanted, acting them out for the animators at Production IG, who had made *Ghost in the Shell* (1995). 'I wanted to have the fun of doing it,'[11] he said, and that was reason enough.

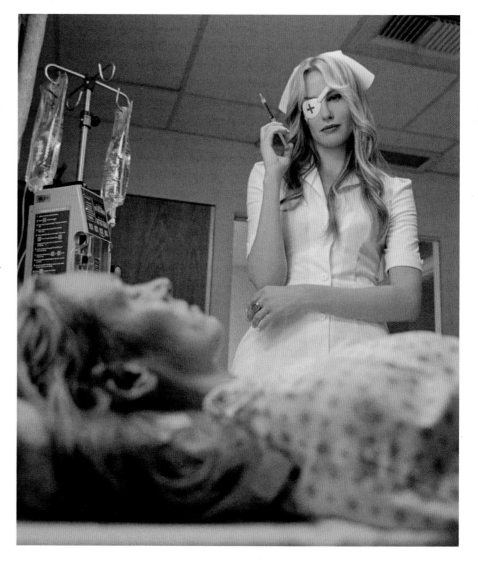

The Quentin Tarantino Archive fansite has established eighty separate films referenced by *Kill Bill Volume 1* from Hitchcock's *Marnie* to retro Japanese horror *Goke, Bodysnatcher from Hell*, from classic Eastern actioners *Lady Snowblood* and *Shogun Assassin* to Ishiro Honda's monster movie *War of the Gargantuas*. Chiba, the Japanese action star of the 1960s who had filled Tarantino's head with visions of samurai cool, makes an extended cameo as droll swordsmith extraordinaire Hattori Hanzo. This is not a reference to the 16th century ninja he played in the television show 'Shadow Warriors'; it is Hanzo, or at least his descendant.

'There's all these Japanese and Chinese things in the movie that I have no expectations that people will get,'[12] delighted Tarantino. Whereas Elle Driver (Hannah's cyclopean sourpuss) was drawn from Swedish thriller *They Call Her One Eye*. 'Of all the revenge movies I've ever seen,' noted the director, 'that is definitely the roughest.'[13]

The referencing game became a hall of mirrors: the black suits worn by O-Ren's private army, the Crazy 88, are not a reference to *Reservoir Dogs*, but a reference to the Japanese schoolchildren death-contest movie *Battle Royale* referencing *Reservoir Dogs*. He was playing on his own magpie reputation. The film was a homage to and exaggeration of the very concept of Quentin Tarantino. If people criticized him for ultraviolence, here was ultra-ultraviolence: symphonic, silly, self-referential and stylized and edited to the frenetic pace of the Shaw Brothers – prodigious producers of kung-fu cinema.

While writing the film, he would watch at least one Shaw Brothers movie a day, if not more, immersing himself in that style of filmmaking until it became second nature.

'I wouldn't have to think about it,' he explained. 'I wouldn't have to be self-conscious about it.'[14]. Using the legendary choreography of Yuen Woo-ping (who had brought his Hong Kong chops to *The Matrix* films), Tarantino would concoct eye-popping fight sequences like musical numbers mixing wushu and kung fu styles, swords and fists, getting down and dirty when required (Fox's character Vernita Green gets skewered through a cereal box). He would throw in crash zooms and fake CGI jets, the whole film unrepentantly self-conscious.

The whole idea on *Kill Bill*, relished Tarantino, was that 'I wanted to see how good I am...'[15]

'He taught himself how to do action for this movie,'[16] added Thurman.

In a mesmerizing, deadpan performance, Thurman could never break cover. She could never wink at the camera, or crack a smile. The Bride's journey would be a gruelling test of icy-calm physical acting, and very real pain. Thurman, in need of her own revival following *The Avengers* and *Batman & Robin*, willingly handed herself over to her director's devilish schemes.

For the fourteen-minute confrontation in the House of Blue Leaves, the climax to *Volume 1* (although, chronologically, the first hit on the list), in which The Bride sees off countless sword-wielding Yakuza while wearing an iconic canary yellow tracksuit identical to that worn by Bruce Lee in *Game of Death*, she went through weeks of training with the samurai and kung fu schools of Chiba and Woo-ping.

Thurman emerged a warrior, able to prepare remarkable six-point moves, only for Tarantino to come in on the day and change his mind. 'That's the kind of person I am,'[17] he giggled. Thurman wasn't fazed, she now had an instinct, and once she practised the new move once or twice, she had it, and they could shoot.

**Above:** Quentin Tarantino plots out another move for the extraordinary fight in the House of Blue Leaves, which took eight weeks to choreograph and shoot. It was full immersion for Tarantino, who had to teach himself how to direct action on this level. Thurman can be seen happily doing the splits on the right of the picture.

I was only safe from stuff I thought an insurance company wouldn't let him do,' she recalled, only half-joking, 'only when it was definitely, positively illegal.'[18]

The sequence took eight weeks to shoot, six weeks longer than had been scheduled. Tarantino was reaching for cinema history; he could already hear the gasps from the aisles. There is not a second of CGI in his epic slaughter house. It was entirely real special effects, exactly as it would have been in the 1970s. This meant fire extinguishers and condoms loaded with blood, loopy wirework and knowingly fake snow begging for bloodstains. Tarantino devised three different variations on the colour of blood to match the hybrid influences – Japanese anime blood, Hong Kong kung fu blood and American exploitation blood – and gave particular attention to the grisly sound effects that come with an eyeball plucking or head slicing.

Right across the film, it was as if his flair for intricate dialogue had been rechannelled into byzantine combat. Characters conversed with violence.

Produced by Lawrence Bender, and backed by a genuflecting Miramax thrilled to have him back behind the camera (although eyebrows began to be raised as he drifted over schedule and over budget, and an expensive moonlit confrontation between The Bride and Bill was abandoned), the bloody saga would shoot for 155 days at a cool $30 million. In fact, so much poured out of Tarantino as he wrote and filmed that he ended up cleaving his new film down the middle and releasing *Kill Bill* in two separate *Volumes* a year apart.

This idea had come from Miramax early in production (the shooting script ran to 222 pages). They could foresee a calamitous edit where Tarantino would be forced into

ditching precious sequences that weren't necessarily driving the plot forward, but were still vital to his conception. Even Tarantino had to admit he 'wouldn't have had the balls'[19] to come out with a four-hour movie. It proved a wise tactic. Not only in doubling the box office potential, but offering two dramatically different but complimentary approaches to the story.

The body count for *Volume 1* is impossible to tally. In the relatively chilled *Volume 2*, only three people shuffle off this mortal coil in front of the camera, although there is live inhumation, two eyeball removals, a snake bite to the face and the slaughter of an entire wedding party (from which the camera discreetly retreats). *Volume 1* is a wanton dance of death without moral consequence, to obscurely hip tunes (Tarantino discovered The 5.6.7.8.'s who even feature live in Oren's club, browsing in a Japanese record store). He could only laugh, relishing the effect. 'The audience and the director, it's an S&M relationship, and the audience is the M. It's exciting! When you go out and have pie afterward, you've got some shit to talk about.'[20]

Whether you bought into it or not, you will be left in no doubt that you had seen a movie. Tarantino was flexing new muscles. If he had flirted with maturity with *Jackie Brown*, he was regressing to full adolescent with *Volume 1*, which manages the paradoxical trick of being wildly inventive, while consciously built from genre conventions like a Lego brick house.

**Right:** Uma Thurman in her element as The Bride, her canary yellow track suit a reference to the one worn by Bruce Lee in Game of Death. Thurman had to train for months beforehand, from nine in the morning until five in the afternoon. Just surviving that, she laughed, was 'empowering.'

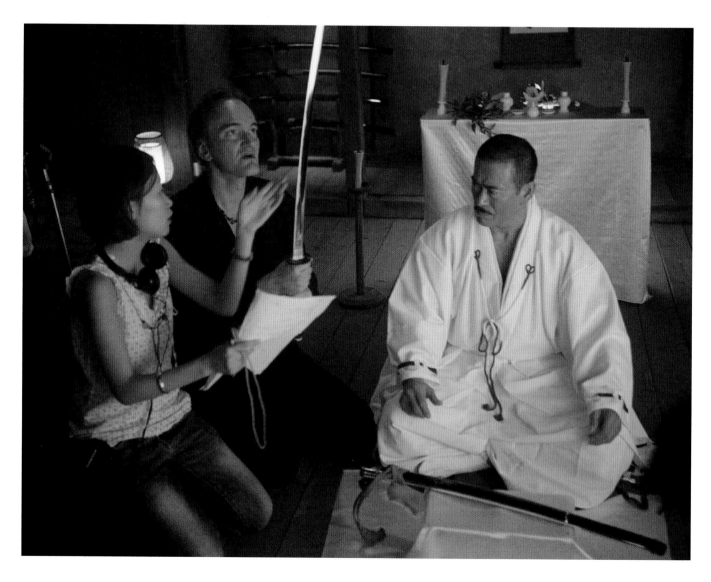

The first film did well enough, making a healthy $70 million, and $181 million worldwide. Though it didn't go unnoticed that this was short of *Pulp Fiction*'s $213 million on a much larger budget. Critics were mostly positive.

The prodigal had returned, with all his rule-breaking nonchalance. They knew where he was coming from. '*Kill Bill: Volume 1* is self-indulgent, overwrought, shallow and ridiculous,' pointed out Rene Rodriguez in the *Miami Herald*, attempting his own Tarantino-style about-face. 'It is also brilliant, a blast of cinematic lunacy.' They could see that it was Tarantino's enthusiasm that holds the whole, uneven spectacle together. As A.O. Scott in *The New York Times* put it, 'the sincerity of his enthusiasm gives this messy, uneven spectacle an odd, feverish integrity.'

There were, of course, those who found it all too much, or not enough. Did it actually mean anything? *Pulp Fiction*, at least, held at its core a sense of lives intersecting and moral dilemmas being confronted. Ed Gonzalez didn't hold back in *Slant* magazine: 'a vacuous junk heap of dorky gags and riffs, violent anime and offensive slapstick.'

Meaning was where *Volume 2* came in.

**Above:** Quentin Tarantino admires the handiwork of Hattori Hanzo. Casting his hero Sonny Chiba as the master swordsmith was a direct tribute to Chiba's 1980s television show 'Shadow Warriors'.

**Above:** Tarantino elaborates on the scene for his leading lady. Uma Thurman became so adept at learning the fight moves, she could swiftly adapt to her director's propensity for changing well-rehearsed sequences on the day of shooting.

'Tarantino would concoct eye-popping fight sequences like musical numbers mixing wushu and kung fu styles.'

If *Volume 1*, with all its grandeur and fury, its exaggerations and jokes, taught the audience the mythology of this world, *Volume 2* was about character. 'The resonance comes in the second half,'[21] confirmed Tarantino. Here is where we would learn the story of The Bride, and her relationship with Bill, and what happened at Two Pines chapel. Here was where all the day-glo mayhem of *Volume 1* would find its emotional consequence.

This was just as Tarantino had intended, a game of two halves: 'If you remember Sonny Chiba's little speech that he gives at the very, very end where he goes, "Revenge is never a straight line, it's a forest. It's easy to get lost and forget where you came in." Well, *Volume 1* is the straight line … Now is the forest. Now the human stuff starts getting in.'[22]

*Volume 2* would largely be set on the fringes of Barstow in the hardscrabble Californian desert where we find Budd (Madsen) working as bouncer in a dead-end topless joint called the My Oh My. For a scene where The Bride, revealed as Beatrix Kiddo, tracks down Bill's old mentor (played by Michael Parks, in a second role, after Ricardo Montalbán turned the film down) in a Mexican whorehouse, Tarantino shot in an authentic whorehouse, complete with Mexican prostitutes. Life was bleeding back into the frame.

It's not as if the film jettisoned its playful martial arts vibe entirely. When The Bride flashbacks – while buried alive in a coffin – to months spent training with the mystical Pai Mei, the almost comical sequence had the heated exaggerations of imported chopsocky films and is bleached out as if the print was faded with overuse (Tarantino abandoned an idea of dubbing Pai Mei's voice himself).

**Above:** After the operatic sequences of The House of Blue Leaves in *Vol. 1*, Tarantino wanted *Vol. 2*'s confrontation between Elle Driver (Daryl Hannah) and The Bride (Uma Thurman) in Bud's cramped trailer to be its polar opposite: a down and dirty 'bitch fight' partly inspired by *Jackass*.

**Opposite:** The Bride is put through her paces by grumpy martial artist Pai Mei (Gordon Liu, taking a second role in the film after playing Crazy 88 leader Johnny in *Vol. 1*) in a flashback sequence in *Vol. 2*. At one point, Tarantino had contemplated doing the voice-over for Pai Mei himself but he ran out of time.

**Right:** David Carradine (as Bill) in conversation with Quentin Tarantino. Once it was decided to split Tarantino's epic script into two volumes, *Vol. 2* took on a markedly different feel to the mania of *Vol. 1*. Here were the emotions, the secret of the past, and the consequences of The Bride's quest for revenge.

*Jackass: The Movie* had squeezed its way into the list of inspirations. The confrontation between Elle and The Bride was wittily conceived to take place within the confines of Budd's ramshackle trailer, which is demolished in the process. There is a terrific running gag that there is never enough room to draw their samurai blades. The sleek moves of *Volume 1* have become an in-joke in its sequel. Tarantino thought of it as the equivalent of the House of Blue Leaves, not in terms of scale, but emotion. He classified it as a 'brutal bitch fight'[23]: Elle is Bill's new lover, The Bride his ex, and arguably true love.

Lingering over real vistas and bathed in sunsets, *Volume 2* is immediately more mythic. 'The best way to describe it is that *Volume 1* is, for lack of a better term, my Eastern with Western influence. *Volume 2* is my Spaghetti Western with an Eastern influence.'[24]

When Tarantino first conceived Bill he looked like Warren Beatty, and he devised an entirely different entrance for the iconic head of the DiVAS. Herein Bill would waltz into a casino carrying a samurai sword, and the security, equipped with blades, would ask him to leave it at the front desk. On reading the script, this mightily confused Beatty.

'Wait a minute; hold it, Quentin. Everybody has a samurai sword?'

'That's the world that this movie takes place in,' replied Tarantino. 'Everybody has a samurai sword.'

'Oh! So this isn't real life?' said Beatty.[25]

In this movie-movie universe, Tarantino told him, people carry samurai swords.

With Beatty in mind, Bill was more of a James Bond character, but Bond as a villain. 'It was playing with Bill as a killer pimp,'[26] enthused Tarantino. However, with Beatty finally getting cold feet (it was claimed he grew twitchy about the level of violence), Tarantino recast and recalibrated the part, adding another layer of reference to the tapestry. David Carradine was best known for the 1970s television series 'Kung Fu', in which he wandered the world righting wrongs (another staple of the young Tarantino's televisual diet). He brought with him, said Tarantino, 'a more mystical quality.'[27]

Carradine had drifted into obscurity, and this was another exercise in career renaissance. He brings an unexpectedly philosophical poise to the titular villain, a character we almost come to like. The film will conclude with that most Tarantino of weapons – conversation. Bill is the source of the single pop cultural symposium in all of *Kill Bill*, when he ponders the existential make-up of Superman.

Superman is different from all other superheroes because when takes his suit off he remains Superman; Clark Kent is who he pretends to be (it is another classic routine mined from Tarantino's Video Archive days). He is attempting to convince his foe that The Bride and Beatrix Kiddo are likewise one and the same. She can never switch off the killer. But in doing so he says more of his own icy heart: 'Clark Kent is Superman's critique of the whole human race …'[28]

During his first experiments with the script, Tarantino had imagined a trilogy of *Kill Bill* movies, the equivalent of the 'Dollars' trilogy, each set ten years apart.

While promoting what had unexpectedly become a double hit, he mentioned the scenario for a possible *Volume 3* set years later, where Nikki (Vernita's young daughter) has grown up and trained, ready to seek her revenge on The Bride.

*Volume 2* was praised for its change of pace and emotional sophistications compared to the action of *Volume 1*. It even reshaped how we viewed the first film. As Michael O'Sullivan pointed out in the *Washington Post* this was 'a love story, darkly, acerbically told, a love story that was only hinted at in *Volume 1*, but that is here filled in with meticulous detail.' *Volume 2* took $66 million in the US ($152 million worldwide) – the two films had done well enough to reaffirm Tarantino's place as a director who could serve his own whims and please a wide audience. There was just a nagging sensation that he was straining – even overcompensating – to write a character that used to come so naturally: Quentin Tarantino.

**Above:** Michael Madsen as Bud in *Vol. 2*. For Madsen the *Kill Bill* films marked a welcome return to the Tarantino world, having missed out on *Pulp Fiction*. He was initially meant to reprise his *Reservoir Dogs* role of Vic Vega only to be delayed making Kevin Costner's *Wyatt Earp*.

# SLASHER MOVIES ARE LEGITIMATE...'

## Grindhouse

t sounded like a sure thing. A gleeful, midnight wheeze catapulted straight from the twinned imaginations of Quentin Tarantino and Robert Rodriguez up onto the screen for the world's delectation. They would join forces on their own Grindhouse spectacular; a double-bill of schlocky horror movies that would pay homage to that particular bandwidth of depraved exploitation cinema they both held dear.

What emerged amid accusations of hubris run amok was Tarantino's first true taste of failure since *Four Rooms*.

While the Sundance gang of 1992 had evaporated, the mutual appreciation society of Tarantino and Rodriguez had continued to flourish. Austin, Texas became Tarantino's 'second home'[1] and whenever Rodriguez was in Los Angeles on business, he got an invitation to his friend's private cinema (where they would later host educational Grindhouse sessions for the cast).

Eager to collaborate again, Rodriguez mentioned an idea that had been bubbling away in his brain for a while. Having successfully revived the dormant 3D format

other lost theatrical experiences and got excited about revisiting the tradition for double-bills of low-grade horror movies. As he initially conceived it, he would direct both, imposing his own budget limitations, serving them up either side of an interval. *Planet Terror*, his variation on the classic zombie movie, would be the first, with the other yet to be determined. At which juncture, he forgot all about it, and went off to make his hyper-stylized noir hit *Sin City*.

Tarantino was sure the tag Grindhouse was coined by the trade bible *Variety*. Film historians point to a 1920s 'grind policy' where theatres offered cut-rate tickets at unsociable hours, but it is generally thought to refer to the dilapidated old picture houses lurking in every town from Austin to

**Above:** Geek buddies Quentin Tarantino and Robert Rodriguez at the Venice Film Festival in 2010. Even after the debacle of *Four Rooms*, they were keen to collaborate again. A mutual love of Grindhouse cinema presented an outrageous possibility

**Above:** Rodriguez had actually conceived of the Grindhouse tribute before being distracted by stylized noir *Sin City*, for which Tarantino directed a single scene as repayment for his friend's contributions to the score for *Kill Bill Vol. 2*.

**Above:** The Grindhouse tradition presented a wealth of poster opportunities for their double bill. In fact, the posters were in effect an extension of the whole Grindhouse experience. But that still failed to attract a wide audience.

Venues that offered their undemanding clientele double and triple bills of Grindhouse genres of every stripe and colour: horror, mob, nudie cuties, Russ Meyer bosom flicks, drugsploitation, carspolitation, Mondo, cannibal, pop samurai, and women in prison movies, to merely scratch the grubby surface.

'You took your life into your own hands,'[2] quipped Rodriguez.

You can guarantee Tarantino, who can see genres beyond the range of normal human reckoning like extra colours in the rainbow, has sought out every single one. His collection of 16mm and 35mm Grindhouse-flavoured prints even included the demented trailers. The best (or worst) of which he saved for Rodriguez whenever he was in town.

So Rodriguez had suggested to his fellow musketeer that they take his double-horror concept up a notch and actually make 'a Quentin night at the movies, but on a grand scale and release it in 3,000 theatres.'[3] It was the ultimate dare, all the gamesmanship of *Kill Bill Volume 1*, but earthbound and scuzzily American. Figuratively speaking, Tarantino and Rodriguez would be inviting fans to The Castle to watch these films alongside them. 'Within five minutes we had the whole idea,'[4] said Rodriguez.

Tarantino saw it as a tribute to loss of those long-disappeared Grindhouses, including the ghetto theatres he frequented as in youth.

In the first flush of excitement, they envisioned it as the start of a franchise.

They could keep going back and trying out another Grindhouse genre for size. Kicking off with horror made the most sense, especially as Rodriguez had thirty pages of zombie infestation already written.

They would confer on their scripts, swapping notes, concocting new plans, although, Rodriguez admitted, more often it was Tarantino suggesting improvements to his script than the other way around. As joint producers, they would consult on casting, and shoot out of Rodriguez's Austin studio facility using much the same crew, one after the other. Tarantino, of course, would also take to the highways of Texas Hill Country and California.

Meantime, *Planet Terror* had mutated from a straightforwardly gross zombie splatter movie into an outright repulsive bio-infection epic, tapping into the Grindhouse ploy of exploiting current

news by tracing the pea-green gas that leaks from a military base back to the Iraq War. The errant chemical will metamorphose an entire town if not into zombies per se, then homicidal bags of pus. Rodriguez was reaching for early John Carpenter (who directed *The Fog* and *The Thing*), even playing the scores from his films on set as mood music.

He would make merry with a big cast, led by a one-legged Rose McGowan as Cherry Darling (who replaces her gnawed-off limb with a machine gun in the film's signature image), and including Josh Brolin, Freddy Rodriguez, Michael Biehn, Jeff Fahey and, briefly, Bruce Willis. In a spirit of self-reference, and positioning both Grindhouse episodes as residents of the same movie-movie universe as *From Dusk Till Dawn* and *Kill Bill* (as opposed to the Tarantino universe of *Pulp Fiction*), both directors brought back

Michael Parks as Sheriff McGraw, along with his son James Parks as Edgar McGraw. We will also meet his daughter: a beautiful if highly strung doctor named Dakota Block-McGraw (Marley Shelton), who has a disturbing bedside manner.

*Planet Terror* shot first, with Rodriguez his usual one-man-band of writer, director, producer, cinematographer, editor and visual effects supervisor. Tarantino, meanwhile, had a blast hanging out on set. He helped coach the actors, lifting spirits with his indefatigable enthusiasm, and was cajoled into operating the second camera in anticipation of being his own cinematographer on *Death Proof*.

During the read-through, he had helpfully filled in as the yet-to-be cast (and motivationally transparent) Rapist No 1, and the cast ended up clamouring for him to take the part. Beaten up by the critics once too often, he admitted he had 'lost the bug to act'[5], but this was irresistible. Echoing the psychotic Richie Gecko in *From Dusk Till Dawn*, showing more than a few signs of contamination, he comes to a (literally) ball-meltingly graphic end, causing squeals of knowing laughter in the stalls.

Rodriguez shot in HD, and then used special effects to scratch up or bleach out the film, and make the audio wonky. The idea was that these were Frankenstein prints made up of different reels that had got beaten up touring the regions. On the Grindhouse circuit, there would rarely be more than five or ten prints made of these pictures; most of those in Tarantino's collection were as dilapidated as the fleapits they once disgraced. 'That becomes part of the experience,'[6] he said. We were to feel as if we were seated in a Grindhouse with its aroma of stale popcorn, worn velour and tacky floors. There would even be missing

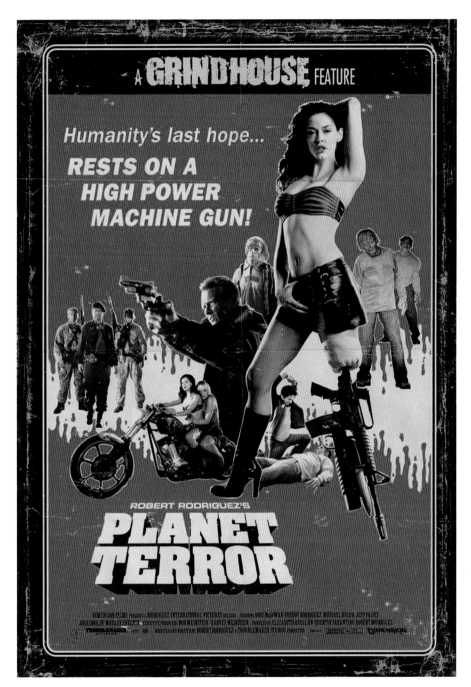

reels (announced by title cards flashed onto the screen) where vital bits of action (or lurid sex scenes) have gone missing, leaving the plot to lurch forwards and us to hastily fill in the gaps.

**Above:** A further poster for *Planet Terror*, Rodriguez's half of the horror double. This gloopy spin on the zombie formula was much closer in spirit, and quality, to what is considered a true Grindhouse movie.

*Planet Terror* pitched its tone at camp splatter. It could easily be condemned as the bloodiest film Tarantino has ever been involved in, if we were required to take it in any way seriously. Which is half its problem: it's one very loud, gross, self-satisfied joke at its own expense. We were held in the orbit of *Kill Bill* by the gravity of Tarantino's passions. Here, outwardly, *Planet Terror* had a throwaway nonchalance that evoked the opposite reaction: it's all a prank.

Between the films came a series of trailers for future presentations that didn't actually exist (at least, at the time) shot by further director friends in on the joke. British director Edgar Wright concocted *Don't!*, a Hammer-like splurge of big house shocks, making sure the British accents cannot be heard (in case they were confusing to an American Grindhouse crowd). Rob Zombie trailed *Werewolf Women of the SS* (featuring Nicolas Cage as Fu Manchu), while Eli Roth (who appears in *Death Proof*) serves up *Thanksgiving* (turkey isn't on the menu). The indefatigable Rodriguez even found the time to tout 'Mexpolitation' thriller *Machete* with Danny Trejo (whom he was so certain was the Mexican Charles Bronson that he went ahead and made the film in 2010). Some screenings also featured a trailer for *Hobo with a Shotgun*, which was the winning entry in a competition set up by Rodriguez and made by a team of unknown Canadian filmmakers (who would transform their vagabond vigilante stinker in a full feature film with Rutger Hauer in 2010).

With horror as their Grindhouse groove of choice, Tarantino had to decide which subgenre of scarefest he wanted to stalk. Having just got through reinvestigating all 'the slasher movies'[7] – this was not an idle boast, he regularly worked his way through entire genres – the choice was easy. 'Slasher movies are legitimate ...' he insisted, and he would do 'his own cockamamie version'[8] of the subgenre just as he had reworked the heist movie with *Reservoir Dogs*. What he liked about slasher movies was also what was so limiting about them: they were basically the same movie every time, which made it a perfect vessel to load up with subtext, but one fixed in its architecture.

His first idea contained the rub of race relations found in his early films (and the kernel of *Django Unchained* to come). A gang of female history students touring the plantations of the Old South would be systematically raped and murdered by the ghost of an old slave known as Jody the Grinder, cursed for having once bested the

Devil (naturally, he was to be played by Samuel L. Jackson). 'How can you not be on the slave's side?'[9] relished Tarantino. But this began to feel too orthodox.

Then he got talking to a stunt man, who told how for $10,000 you could 'death proof'[10] any car to ensure the driver survived even head-on collisions.

'What if this guy uses a car?' he wondered. 'And what if his thing is to follow girls who travel in a posse?'[11] He pictured a demented stuntman (whose career was on the skids),

who had a death-proof car, and slaughtered females in 'accidents' for the sexual kicks the subgenre required. 'What he was doing was a rape-murder,'[12] concluded Tarantino.

It was a slasher movie he could coat in a veneer of film history: the long, twisted vault of great car chases.

'This was the first time since *Reservoir Dogs*, I had come up with an idea and just sat down and wrote it,'[13] he claimed. The impulsive nature of it all was thrilling. It took him four months to get from a blank page to

a finished script, in which he subverted the slasher rulebook, creating as much a study in female empowerment as carsploitation junk. There was nothing hokey or cheesy or drippy in his film.

**Above:** Robert Rodriguez shot his Grindhouse epic in and around his base in Austin. While shooting using state-of-the-art digital cameras, he employed visual effects to make the image look scratched and warped from too many projections.

**Above:** The first of the two girl gangs featured in *Death Proof*. Eli Roth pictured in the centre wearing a red T-shirt was another fellow director who not only cameoed, but provided one of the fake trailers in *Thanksgiving*. He would later star as one of the *Inglourious Basterds*. The jukebox is Quentin Tarantino's own.

The two girl gangs we meet – Mk I (Sydney Poitier, Vanessa Ferlito, Jordan Ladd and Marcy Harriell); Mk II (Zoë Bell, Tracie Thoms, Rosario Dawson and Mary-Elizabeth Winstead; Rose McGowan, in a markedly different role, crosses over from *Planet Terror* to become the first victim) evoke the familiar, easy interactions of real life. *Death Proof* is talkative, even for Tarantino. The girls chat and chat, at home (where Poitier lounges on a sofa beneath a giant print of Brigitte Bardot) and in Warren's Bar, where

the titular barkeep (providing another cameo from his truly) serves up swigs of Chartreuse. The jukebox was shipped to set direct from The Castle in LA.

For five years Tarantino had been hanging with different posses of female friends, the only guy along for the ride. He had come to enjoy their group dynamic better than its male iteration. 'I got the chance to say all their funniest lines,' he admitted, 'and a couple of girls are based on girls in particular.'[14] He didn't want them

sounding antiquated like old Tarantino characters. There would be none of those backward-glancing cultural digressions. He wanted them to feel authentic, jockeying for position, bemoaning guys, confident in expressing themselves. But they never quite generated the same crackle of personality as his early films.

Ferlito's Butterfly represents a classic case of inverting the conventions of the slasher movie. Everything about the film, acknowledged Tarantino, suggested she

would be the 'final girl'[15]: she's the odd one out among her friends, the one who senses the evil in Stuntman Mike, spots his car. Then Tarantino makes one of his left-hand swerves when she is taken out in the terrifying head-on collision (one of the most brutal scenes he has ever shot, playing in real time and then reversing to show how each individual girl is killed in agonizing slow-motion). Even though we had all the warning in the world – this was Grindhouse – the effect is traumatizing. You can't trust

what the director might do next. Whatever madcap mood had clung on from *Planet Terror* is shattered.

**Above:** Cherry Darling (Rose McGowan) and Dr Dakota Block (Marley Shelton) posed on a chopper for a publicity shot for *Planet Terror*. McGowan would be the only star to take a specific role in both films.

True to the Tarantinoesque spirit, despite being contemporary, he thought of *Death Proof* as the kind of film he might have made in the 1970s – an unfamiliar thriller like *The Candy Snatchers* (teen-heiress kidnap witnessed by abused autistic boy) or *Macon County Line* (sheriff hunts down vagrants who killed his wife). Rodriguez was giddy with the news that Tarantino was thinking of casting Kurt Russell as Stuntman Mike. There had been brief mention of Mickey Rourke, whom Tarantino had loved in *Sin City* (they were also extracurricular buddies), but Russell

was the poker-faced icon of Carpenter greats like *The Thing* and *Escape from New York*. 'It was like he was hiding in plain sight,' recalled Tarantino, 'and I was like, "Oh man that's totally what I gotta do, that's the guy!!"'[16]

Additionally, Tarantino liked how he had begun as a child actor and ground out a career the hard way. 'There's a wonderful aspect that Kurt has that's fantastic, and it mirrors Stuntman Mike a lot. He's a working professional and he's been in this business for a long time. He's done all this episodic television – he did all those

TV series, 'The High Chaparrals' and the 'Harry O's'. And he's worked with fucking everybody. Literally. So he knows the life that Stuntman Mike's had.'[17]

Russell could also handle himself behind the wheel of either of the two death-proofed killer-cars: a 1970 Chevy Nova and a 1969 Dodge Charger. For all its initial talk (and the first hour would have bugged the heck out of a Grindhouse crowd in its heyday), *Death Proof* follows *Kill Bill* as another experiment in the tropes of action.

Having real stuntwomen playing themselves (fictionally, they are working for

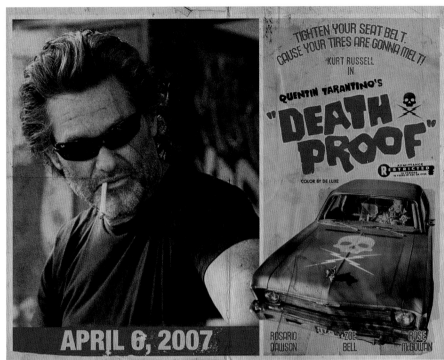

APRIL 6, 2007

**Left:** Automotive slaughter – Tarantino had always wanted to make a classic car chase movie as well as try a slasher film. With *Death Proof* he got to combine both celluloid peccadillos.

**Above:** Another variation on the poster for *Death Proof* featuring star Kurt Russell. In a sense Tarantino would break his own rules, making a tribute to the slasher movie without any deliberate hokiness. In fact, it was more in keeping with a 'Tarantino movie' than a 'Grindhouse flick'.

a nearby movie shoot), in Thoms and Bell (who was Uma Thurman's stunt double in *Kill Bill*), allowed Tarantino to simply play everything for real (with no CGI tinkering). With Bell strapping herself to the bonnet of their 1970 Dodge Challenger (from car classic *Vanishing Point*) for kicks before Stuntman Mike begins a battle of automotive wits.

Premiered on 26 March 2007, critics expressed their misgivings about the whole *Grindhouse* attitude. Regular Tarantino-advocate Roger Ebert in the *Chicago Sun-Times* was amused, but could see that 'its standing in the canon of the two directors'

was minor. Unlike *Kill Bill Volume 1* (which added up to more than the sum of its exploitative parts), it is unclear if these were to be taken as Grindhouse-level films, or if they were sending them up.

There is no doubt that they genuinely wanted the audience to join in their celebration of trash, but this assumed we were automatically on their wavelength. The conceit itself was the content, and many watchers were left cold. For all the gloopy horrors, *Planet Terror* was a hypothetical exercise. *Death Proof* wears better, but at three hours and eleven minutes, the

entire nutso-nostalgic Grindhouse pastiche swiftly loses its quirky appeal. There was a suspicion that by embracing gonzo moviemaking, Tarantino and Rodriguez were relinquishing their responsibility towards their own talents. 'At a certain point, of course, a loving re-creation of something tawdry isn't all that different from the original,' observed David Denby in *The New Yorker*. 'Even a postmodernist bloodbath is wet, sticky, and red.'

Devoted fans dutifully joined in, whooping and hollering on cue (it demanded audience participation). But as Tarantino remorsefully admitted, they only got a Friday night. For once, his elevation of his own cult predilections fell flat. Their midnight plotting awoke to the morning after as they bombed in America making only $25 million (on a budget of $67 million – paradoxically ersatz dirt-cheap schlockers didn't come cheap). A rethink was required for its international roll out.

Miramax had already established plans to release the two films separately in foreign territories where the Grindhouse tradition didn't translate, nor even the notion of a double-bill. These would be longer, less deviant (no missing reels or combustible frames) versions of each film. They effectively made three different movies: *Planet Terror*, *Death Proof* and *Grindhouse*. With its box office implosion, the films were also separated for territories. In some, still due to be in on the joke, the whole *Grindhouse* affair was left for DVD.

Tarantino was not completely averse to the change of plan. Freed from its gimmicky berth, *Death Proof* could relax back into the Tarantino movie it unmistakably wanted to be. He admitted how much he had hated cutting it down to fit the double-bill. He had to 'demolish strategies'[18] he had worked really hard to get into the piece. It had felt counterintuitive. Twenty-seven additional minutes were re-inserted (including the 'missing' lap dance sequence) and what emerged was the Fifth Film by Quentin Tarantino: another smart, character-driven reworking of genre absolutely of a part with his previous four films, but not the tomfoolery of *Planet Terror*. Irony didn't suit Tarantino.

He even chose to debut this stand-alone cut at Cannes, thrilling to the sound of screams from an audience dressed in ball gowns and penguin suits.

**Opposite:** Quentin Tarantino in consultation with Kurt Russell as the sinister Stuntman Mike. Look closely and you will see that Tarantino is wearing a bespoke Grindhouse T-shirt in the style of rock band AC/DC, only the lettering says RR/QT.

**Above:** Freddy Rodriguez as hero El Wray negotiates a burning hospital in *Planet Terror*. Rodriguez was playing homage to his great horror hero John Carpenter, something that was underlined in the casting of Carpenter's leading man Kurt Russell in *Death Proof*.

YOU MIGHT FEEL A LITTLE PRICK.

ROBERT RODRIGUEZ'S
PLANET TERROR
APRIL 6, 2007

'One of those out-of-touch, old, limp, flaccid-dick movies costs you three good movies as far as your rating is concerned.'

— Quentin Tarantino

**Left:** Before their high-concept double bill flopped, Rodriguez and Tarantino envisioned Grindhouse as a potential franchise to which they could return every few years and experiment with a new subgenre.

**Opposite:** A publicity shot of Tarantino as the barman Warren decanting Chartreuse into a boot-shaped glass. Once the films had been split for foreign release, Tarantino took great delight in unveiling his new, extended cut of *Death Proof* amongst all the arty films at the Cannes Film Festival.

'I learned a big lesson with *Grindhouse,* and I try not to repeat the mistake. Robert Rodriguez and I had gotten used to going our own way, on these weird roads, and having the audience come along. We'd started thinking they'd go wherever we wanted. With *Grindhouse*, that proved not to be the case. It was still worth doing, but it would have been better if we weren't caught so unaware by how uninterested people were.'[19] In retrospect, Tarantino has come to view *Death Proof* (a little unfairly) as his least effective film. It's a relative distinction, of course. 'If that's the worst I ever get, I'm

good,'[20] he reflected. But warning had been served that he was not a movie Midas, and it affirmed a growing desire not to allow his career to drift into mediocrity. He was going to fulfil his promise and then retire. He feared the gradual ebbing of his talents: those last few films that leave the critics shaking their heads. 'One of those out-of-touch, old, limp, flaccid-dick movies costs you three good movies as far as your rating is concerned.'[21]

He began dropping hints that he would call time on his career once he had reached ten films.

'I don't intend to be making movies deep into my old age,' he confessed. 'I don't really want to be a geriatric filmmaker. I'm thinking about fans that are not even born, when they are like me when I was fourteen and I discovered Howard Hawks.'[22]

If so, he was halfway to the end of this career.

# 'JUST FUCKING KILL HIM.'

## Inglourious Basterds

Back in the Video Archives days, whenever the gang got talking about
their favourite World War II men-on-a-mission movies – a classic subgenre
including such luminaries as *The Dirty Dozen* and *The Guns of Navarone*,
but, as Quentin Tarantino would keenly point out, also including an entire
regiment of neglected gems – they would refer to them under the catch-all
term of Inglorious Bastards movies.

The term was in honour of Enzo Castellari's *The Inglorious Bastards*, in their eyes one of the greats. Starring blaxploitation icon Fred Williamson, this 1978 macaroni combat (a sub-subgenre) flick followed the escapades of a gang of black soldiers who abscond from a court martial to do their unconventional bit for the war effort.

Stirred by nostalgia, in the wake of *Jackie Brown* Tarantino bought the rights to Castellari's film with the idea of lifting that tale, reworking it somehow, and seeing where the characters might take him. He had often professed that a men-on-a-mission movie was high on his to-do list. Tinkering with genre was his creative foundation stone, but the six-year hiatus that swelled between *Jackie Brown* and *Kill Bill* can be partly accounted for by the fact he couldn't

stop writing 'his bunch of guys on a mission thing.'[1] It was turning into a gargantuan novel more than a movie, much like *The Open Road* years before: 500 pages long, with enough material for three movies.

If anything, he confessed, he had become too inspired. His brain kept inventing new ideas, new characters and new twists on convention. He began to worry that movies were no longer big enough to contain his vision. And once he returned from *Kill Bill* (which had barely been contained by two films), with unwitting foresight he contemplated turning his script into a miniseries.

'I was going to follow the original story about American troops escaping while being convoyed to court martial and execution. It was going to be my first original script after *Pulp Fiction*.'[2]

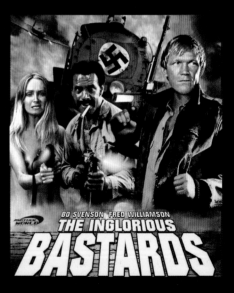

**Above:** The poster for the original *Inglorious Bastards*, a macaroni men-on-a-mission epic that Quentin Tarantino once contemplated remaking in his own style, only to take his own devious, incorrectly spelled, *Inglourious Basterds* route.

**Previous page:** As he was writing his World World II epic, Tarantino had imagined that he might fill the role of Aldo Raine, part-Apache leader of the Inglourious Basterds brigade. However, once he envisaged Brad Pitt in the role, there was no looking back.

**Right:** A trio of *Inglourious Basterds*: Samm Levine, Til Schweiger and Eli Roth. Tarantino wanted to emphasize that this vengeful unit was not simply Jewish, but entitled Jewish – they had the entire American nation behind them.

By chance, he had dinner with his friend French director Luc Besson, and they got talking about future plans. Besson was aghast at the suggestion Tarantino might decamp to television. He remonstrated with his friend that his name was one of the few things that made him go to the cinema. That struck home – the Church of Cinema must remain sacrosanct, and he began to toy with ways of cutting it back into a movie.

Rethinking his central conceit, an alternative, inglorious concept took shape. 'I was coming up with the idea of the American Jews taking vengeance,'[3] he said. He tried it out on his Jewish friends, the notion of a renegade gang of Jewish soldiers behind enemy lines taking the fight to the Nazis. He was testing the waters on how far he could conceivably push things. They were unanimous – where do we sign up?

What would emerge is one of Tarantino's most daring and exhilarating films. A film that confirmed that he was far more than the figurehead of a flurry of a punk-like fervour at the beginning of the 1990s. With *Kill Bill* and *Grindhouse* there was a suspicion he would end up simply circling his own reputation, rather than enhancing it. Quite against even Miramax's most optimistic expectations, *Inglourious Basterds*, with $321 million worldwide, would be his biggest hit to date.

He has dropped hints that he may return to the original conception one day with a script now liberated from *Inglourious Basterds* and rechristened *Killer Crows*. Incidentally, the title, with its conscious misspelling, was either just that (Tarantino's dire spelling, which he found amusing enough to keep), a way of differentiating it from the original, or an artistic flourish that, like any meaning behind *Reservoir Dogs*, he wasn't willing to explain. Would you ask why Picasso used his brush in a particular way?

Now clear in his purpose, the characters began to suggest actors to him. Each one, he knew, had to be a home run.

At one time Tarantino contemplated himself as Lieutenant Aldo Raine, the leader of the Basterds (Raine's half-native, hillbilly background is a joke at his own expense). But as the script progressed he had to admit that Aldo was closer in looks to Brad Pitt. In fact, he looked *exactly* like Brad Pitt. He and Pitt had met and expressed their mutual appreciation and desire to work together (Pitt, of course, having already had a taste of Tarantino's worldview clamped to the sofa in *True Romance*), but it required the right moment, the right set of clothes. Once he couldn't picture anyone else, Tarantino knew he was in trouble.

He had a month in which to land his leading man before rehearsals began, and he was certain the reputedly fussy superstar would have three movies already lined up in his diary. 'So it was a perfect storm of no,'[4] he groaned. Pitt, it turned out, liked to keep his options open, for exactly this kind of chance opportunity.

'At the end of the day this is a director's medium,'[5] he iterated, and Tarantino was a rare commodity.

The Greatest High Adventure Ever Filmed!

COLUMBIA PICTURES presents

GREGORY PECK | DAVID NIVEN | ANTHONY QUINN

in CARL FOREMAN'S

THE GUNS OF NAVARONE

co-starring
STANLEY BAKER · ANTHONY QUAYLE · IRENE PAPAS · GIA SCALA and JAMES DARREN

Written & Produced by CARL FOREMAN | Based on the novel by ALISTAIR MacLEAN | Music Composed & Conducted by DIMITRI TIOMKIN | Directed by J. LEE THOMPSON | A HIGHROAD PRESENTATION | COLOR and CINEMASCOPE

**Above:** J. Lee Thompson's 1961 hit *The Guns of Navarone* is considered the embodiment of the men-on-a-mission subgenre, featuring a group of disparate, but skilled, individuals assembled to take on a high-risk mission behind enemy lines.

There followed a night at Pitt's French estate, wine was taken, stories swapped and the actor, irrespective of whether he could pin down the point he said yes or not, awoke the following morning as Aldo Raine.

Raine actually predated *Inglourious Basterds*. He was floating around Tarantino's imagination even before *Reservoir Dogs*. By the time he was writing his World War II epic, he had an entire backstory at the ready (true of many of his major characters). 'Aldo had been fighting racism in the South,' he explained; 'he was fighting the Klan before he ever got to World War II.'[6] He was half-Apache, and Tarantino was drawing parallels between genocides. 'The fact that Aldo is part Indian,' he iterated, 'is a very important part of my whole conception.'[7] Raine and his men graphically scalp their victims, which Tarantino reveals in all its unflinching horror.

The gang he commands, however, is made up of those vengeful Jews. Like *Kill Bill*, his new film was on one level a rip-roaring rampage of revenge. That brash Grindhouse sensibility wasn't completely out of his system either. Here too were classic Tarantino themes: professionalism, loyalty, betrayal, race and the wages of violence.

Pitt was also encouraged that while his would be the jutting chin on which the film was sold, it was very much an ensemble piece whose different strands ingeniously intertwine over five chapters. Much like *Pulp Fiction*, Pitt was impressed how it felt more like a novel, going heartbeat by heartbeat through certain scenes (usually seated around a table), while bypassing acres of formulaic backstory. The adventure story, according to Tarantino's designation, only swings into action in the final two chapters, with the first three of his instinctive subdivisions (the first two remaining much

**Right:** Quentin Tarantino on the set of *Inglourious Basterds* in Germany. The director was determined not to trap his film in a stifling period bubble. He was influenced by the style of wartime propaganda movies, which were deliberately contrived to be thrilling adventures.

**Opposite:** Finding the perfect slippery, eloquent, conniving Colonel Landa was integral to the film working. Tarantino had been on the verge of abandoning the project entirely when Christoph Waltz walked through his door.

as they had been written ten years before) there to introduce us to the three contrasting protagonists: Raine, and his ardent band of Nazi scalpers; Shosanna, the runaway Jew and her Paris cinema; and Jew hunter Colonel Hans Landa, thrilling to the sound of his own silken wit.

A perfect Landa was even more imperative than a fitting Raine. Tarantino knew he was one of the best characters he had ever written. Born of a long line of suave Hollywood Nazis (George Sanders and Claude Raines are touchstones), he also shares that classically Tarantino pleasure in circumlocution with Jules from *Pulp Fiction*. Dallying over syllables as if savouring their taste. He had been written as a linguistic genius, a Video Archives smart alec with ice in his veins, and the actor needed to be a linguistic genius to deliver those lines. And having tried what seemed like every

actor in Germany, he still hadn't appeared. Tarantino was willing to abandon the film entirely if he remained elusive.

Then, in a stroke of fortune, Christoph Waltz strolled into his life.

Born in Vienna, he had worked his way up through German theatre into a steady career of television and films without managing that precious breakthrough into English language films. The triumvirate of Tarantino, Landa and *Inglourious Basterds* would bring Waltz a Best Supporting Actor Oscar and an introduction to Hollywood. He never looked back. It was all about the characters, Tarantino insisted. It was they who demand he reinvent a career or, in this case, invent a career. Gliding over two scenes with that lovely, rhythmic delivery (he is like an aristocratic Christopher Walken), Tarantino's heart rose. As Waltz left, he turned to Bender and

grinned his crazy, lopsided grin: 'We've got a movie.'[8] They high fived.

Tarantino ran a film class for all his cast members, schooling them in the finer points of World War II cinema. For Mélanie Laurent as Shosanna (his most understated character since Jackie Brown), this not only meant a list of films she should watch, but the *specific* films he considered to be Shosanna's top ten. Into Shosanna's Parisian arthouse will fall the premiere of a new (fictional) German propaganda film (*Nation's Pride* – shot in its entirety by friend and director Eli Roth, who also rises to the occasion as the baseball bat-wielding Basterd Donny Donowitz) and the opportunity to strike at the heart of the enemy, with Hitler and a top ten of Nazi bigwigs due to attend.

**Above:** A posed shot of French actress Mélanie Laurent as escapee Jewish girl Shosanna against the despised Swastika. The daubs of red make-up hint at war paint and Tarantino's subtextual connection of World War II with the genocide of Native Americans. Brad Pitt's character Aldo Raine, we learn, is half-Apache.

In this mix of real figures (we also briefly meet Rod Taylor's Winston Churchill) and fictional ones (and with a hook of the familiar, Samuel L. Jackson narrates) Tarantino was eagerly transgressing yet another borderline (although, didn't all war movies do that to a certain degree?).

If Pitt had any misgivings about jumping on this runaway train, it wasn't the mad rush into production so much as the tone of the ending. Were they really going to change the course of history? Was it something you

could tastefully get away with? He could picture the backlash.

Tarantino had explained that when following the lead of his characters, there are certain roadblocks you come up against. 'In this instance,' he said, 'one of the big roadblocks was history itself.'[9] Pitt was reassured that his director had done his homework, both filmic (of course) and factual (he revealed an impressive command of World War II minutiae). If his film was about to play extremely fast and lose with

the historical record, it was doing so very consciously. All the same, Tarantino had been as surprised as anyone that he ended up killing Hitler (and the upper echelons of the Nazi party) in a burning cinema.

'That wasn't the jumping-off point for the film,'[10] he admitted. It was the only way past the roadblock. He had been writing all day, by hand as always, raiding his vinyl collection for inspirational music (mainly, his musical god, Ennio Morricone) and was meditating over the inconvenience of

history. 'Finally I just grabbed a pen, went over to a piece of paper and wrote, "Just fucking kill him." I put it near my bedside table so I would see it when I woke up the next morning and could decide after a night's sleep if it was still a good idea. I saw it, paced around awhile and said, "Yeah, that's a good idea."'[11]

Naturally, he already knew of a movie precedent: a 1942 propaganda thriller called *Hitler–Dead or Alive* about a rich guy who offers a million-dollar bounty on Hitler's

life, and three gangsters who come up with a plan to off the Führer. 'It's a wacky movie that goes from being serious to very funny. The gangsters get Hitler, and when they start beating the fuck out of him, it is just so enjoyable.'[12]

**Above:** Sgt Donny Donowitz (Eli Roth) and Lt Aldo Raine (Brad Pitt) prepare to scalp an enemy soldier. *Inglourious Basterds* was an emphatic statement that Quentin Tarantino was getting more daring with age. Where once he had turned away from an ear slicing, he shows the scalping in all its graphic detail.

**Above:** Movies at war – undercover film critic Lt Archie Hicox (Michael Fassbender) makes contact with double-agent actress Bridget von Hammersmark (Diane Kruger). The incredibly tense cellar bar sequence features pretend Germans playing a card game that ironically involves them pretending to be famous movie stars.

In preparation for his own take on the sub-sub-subgenre of killing Hitler movies, rather than the usual parade of men-on-a-mission staples he knew backwards, he immersed himself in propaganda movies made in the 1940s by émigré masters like Fritz Lang (*Man Hunt*), Jules Dassin (*Reunion in France*) and Jean Renoir (*This Land Is Mine*). What struck him was that they had been made literally in the shadow of the Nazi threat. 'Yet these movies are entertaining, they're funny, there's humor in them … They're allowed to be thrilling adventures.'[13]

It was a form of defiance.

Furthermore, *Inglourious Basterds* isn't simply a film depicting Hitler's demise, the orgasmic deluge of death at the finale is contained within a cinema (it is a rare film that shows how film is threaded into a projector), and film is the medium by which death is delivered (Shosanna uses highly flammable film stock to burn the building down). Cinema, you could say, is righting history. It is a theme Tarantino has alluded to before: in *Kill Bill* only when The Bride enacts the rituals of martial arts cinema can she right the wrongs of the universe, while in *Death Proof* it takes a stunt-team – real movie people played by real movie people –

to stop the killer. We also meet Archie Hicox (Michael Fassbender, a sterling replacement for Simon Pegg), a peacetime film critic turned lantern-jawed undercover British agent, fluent in German cinema.

As the shoot progressed, Pitt found himself not only won over by their outrageous conceit, but a zealot for its cathartic power. This was almost like science fiction, one of those alternative universe pictures where time runs askew.

After *Kill Bill* and *Death Proof*, the grand, period setting of *Inglourious Basterds* firmly established Tarantino's reach far beyond the city limits of Los Angeles. If *Pulp Fiction* channelled a European view of American culture, *Inglourious Basterds* voiced an American view of Europe (there is a fabulous moment when a supposedly undercover Raine attempts a Dixie variation on '*buon giorno*', and Pitt maintains a jubilant comic timbre throughout). Across the latter half of 2008, they shot, at pace, on location in Paris, the lush scenic countryside of Saxony and at the fabled Studio Babelsberg in Berlin, where Goebbels once marshalled his propaganda machine.

Purposefully crossing his genres, Tarantino was making another Spaghetti Western by stealth. The glorious opening

**Above:** At first Tarantino had worried he was pushing taste too far with the idea of American Jews taking vengeance in Nazi-occupied Paris. But when he tested his concept on Jewish friends, he got a resounding chorus of approval. They very much wanted to see this story.

vistas are of a kind we had never seen before in his work. 'I remember when I first started this movie after *Jackie Brown*, one of the things I wanted it to be was my *The Good, The Bad and The Ugly*,'[14] he said, noting that Sergio Leone's American Civil War classic, with its balance of irony and tradgedy, was now fixed as his favourite film.

Shortly before he died, Leone was about to begin his own World War II war story on Stalingrad, and the Italian maestro's operatic sensibility is honoured in the title given to the first chapter, 'Once Upon a Time in Nazi-Occupied France...'[15], which introduces us to Landa, his nose virtually quivering at the scent of a Jewish family hidden beneath the floorboards of a French farmhouse. Here too is the tenor of a fairy tale, as a distraught Shosanna flees for her life, leaving behind a shoe. And what is the film if not wish fulfilment?

Nevertheless, after the soul-sapping overthinking of *Grindhouse* and *Kill Bill*'s delirious extravagancies, Tarantino refused himself the space for any form of self-indulgence. He set Cannes as his deadline, determined to finish his film in under a year in order to make the festival the following spring. If the schedule enforced a single day to get a shot, so be it. He wanted to test himself again, regain the urgency of his early work. Filmed largely in sequence, the tension gradually builds like a grip tightening on a throat, as both the mission and the tonal gamble of the filmmaking threaten to fall apart.

Tarantino's didn't want to do battle scenes – 'That shit bores me'[16] – such formulaic war-movie paraphernalia bored him. No, this was to be about human frictions, 'the stuff in rooms.'[17] He wanted to stretch what he called the 'rubber band'[18] within a scene as far as he could without it snapping. Instead of gunfire (at least until Chapter Five, Revenge of the Giant Face) characters would negotiate the tripwire of language.

'It's one of the reasons I can direct my material better than anyone else,' said Tarantino, 'because I have a confidence in my material that no one else would.'[19]

Chapter Four, Operation Kino, set at a cellar bar named La Louisiane, is a tour de force of sustained directorial control, and among his greatest achievements. Across a single scene stretched agonizingly taut over thirty minutes, a gaggle of drunken German soldiers threatens to expose the rendezvous between select Basterds, Hicox and a wonderful Diane Kruger as Bridget von Hammersmark, a German movie star turned Allied agent who will provide the means of entry into the forthcoming premiere. It all comes down to a matter of pronunciation and gesture.

amusing to see choice Tarantino dialogue relayed as subtitles.

Finishing the film with hours to spare (he would actually go back and tighten up the edit following its debut), the film received a mixed reception in Cannes in 2009. The tone did worry some critics, but it was more the arrogance that he would even dare such a story that seemed to irk the naysayers. 'At this point in his career, frankly, it feels like his personality is stronger than his films,' grumbled Kenneth Turan in the *Los Angeles Times*. Tarantino was being shot down for being Tarantino. Which for others was still exactly what dazzled: 'Tarantino rewrites history with the only authority he has: his sovereignty as a filmmaker,' confirmed Peter Travers in *Rolling Stone*. 'The notion is as intoxicating as it is demented,' added Philip French in *The Observer*.

By the time *Inglourious Basterds* launched in America in the summer of 2009, the matter was settled. Eight Oscar nominations followed, including Best Picture, Best Original Screenplay and that victory for Waltz as Best Supporting Actor. Tarantino could dare the impossible. So next he turned his eyes towards the small matter of a full-blown Western, and tackling slavery.

More than ever, this is a return to *Pulp Fiction*'s deft exploration of language. It is now one of the principal themes. Not only through the purring, polyglot genius of Landa, Tarantino also recognized that to sustain a disguise in the theatre of war, or simply grasp an enemy command, language was a matter of life and death. So he was determined to cast exactly by nationality (German actors as Germans etc – with the exception of the Canadian Mike Myers as a 'pip-pip' English general, and an Irishman in Fassbender as Hicox). Each national would speak in their own tongue, and it is

# '...the orgasmic deluge of death at the finale is contained within a cinema ... and film is the medium by which death is delivered.'

**Right:** Shosanna (Mélanie Laurent) surveys the gathering of Nazi bigwigs and society guests about to be trapped in her Paris cinema. Not only was Quentin Tarantino rewriting history in a movie, he was using a cinema as the very means by which he would bring about Hitler's downfall and death.

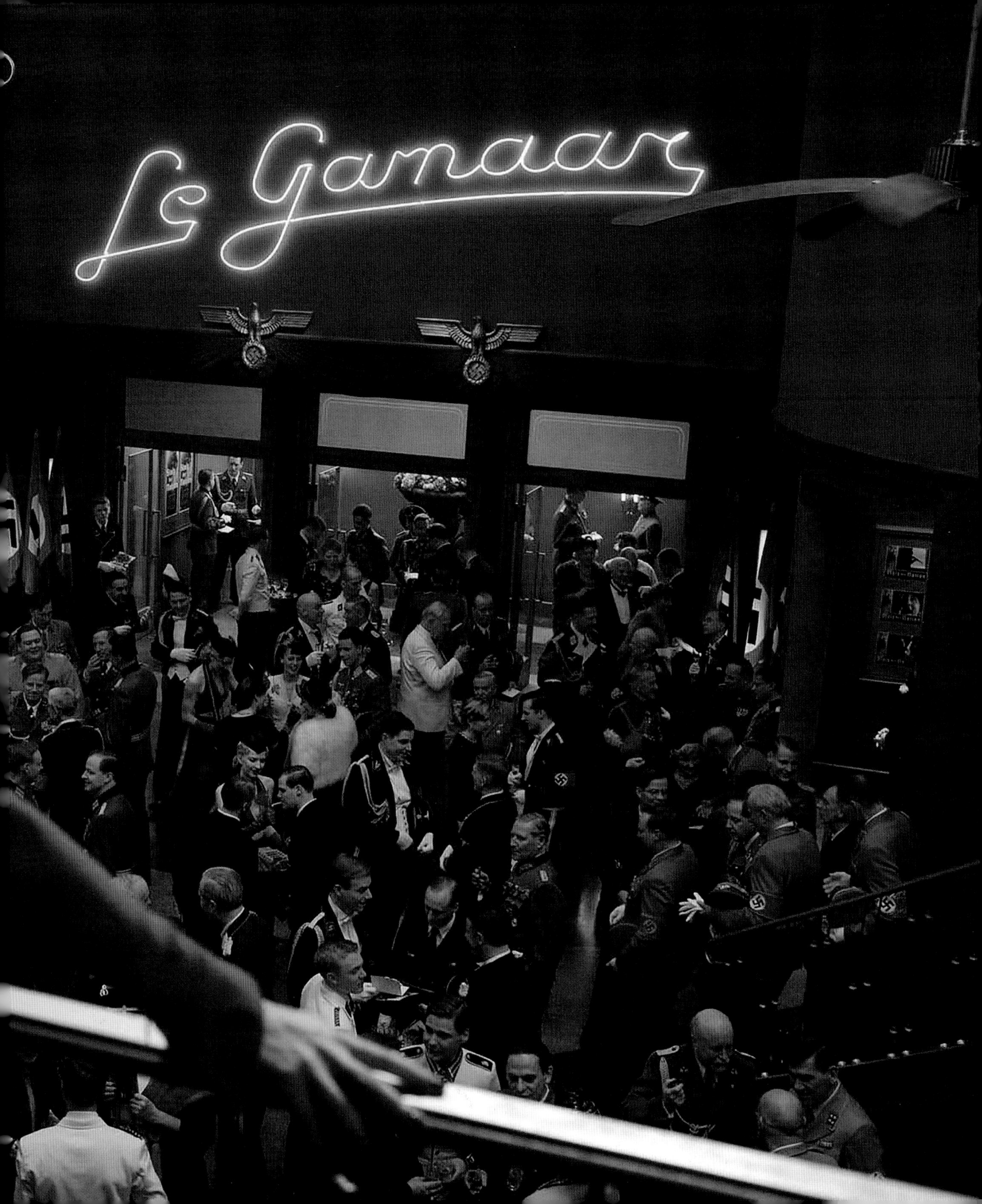
Le Gamaar

# 'LIFE IS CHEAP. LIFE IS DIRT. LIFE IS A BUFFALO NICKEL.'

## Django Unchained

The muse alighted on him on the Japanese leg of the press tour for *Inglourious Basterds*. Whatever the exact source of inspiration might be – God, the universe, the collective subconscious of movie history whispering in his ear – Quentin Tarantino can trace the spark behind the opening scene of his next film to a set of obscure Spaghetti Western soundtracks he found in a Tokyo record store.

Spaghettis, with their co-option of samurai mythology, are big in Japan. Tarantino spent his day off listening to the scores, and an opening scene took shape in his imagination. In a rare instance caught without his notebooks, he began scribbling it down on hotel stationery before it got away.

Exterior. Night. 1858 – somewhere in Texas. In a freezing wood, a line of slaves, shackled by the ankle, emerge out of the mist to be confronted by a German bounty hunter disguised as a dentist. This charming man, as fond of his own voice as anyone in the history of Tarantino chatterboxes, is seeking one slave in particular. He goes by the name of Django.

Tarantino had already decided upon a Western. The genre had been calling to him his whole career as he infiltrated other species of movie with the tropes of his

beloved Spaghettis. What finally persuaded him to try one outright was the book of subtextual criticism on Spaghetti princeling Sergio Corbucci (director of the 1966 *Django*) that he was writing in his spare time. What was great about going subtextual, he said, was that it didn't matter if Corbucci actually intended any of his findings as long 'as you made your case.'[1]

The best Westerns were always defined by their maker, be it Anthony Mann or Sam Peckinpah or Sergio Leone. Corbucci's depiction of the West was the most brutal and surreal of all. Tarantino's theory was that the Italian director was actually processing the Fascism that had plagued his country during World War II. That got him thinking: what might some future critic write about Quentin Tarantino's West? So he decided to find out.

**Above:** For his first bona fide Western, Quentin Tarantino was inspired by the work of Italian Spaghetti maestro Sergio Corbucci, in particular his riotous 1966 work *Django*, in which a slick gunslinger takes revenge on a gang of Confederate swine.

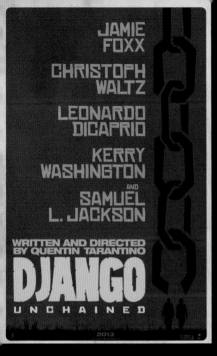

The idea of the freed slave working as a bounty hunter had been in the incubator for eight years, this angel of vengeance who tracked down outlaws hiding in plain sight as overseers on the cotton plantations of the Deep South. Research had revealed how scum with a price on their head often hid out on the remote estates of the South. Tarantino liked to refer to his seventh film as a 'Southern'.

His current actor of choice, Christoph Waltz, was the final piece of the puzzle. Dr King Schultz, the bounty hunter who becomes a mentor and friend to Django, was shaped around the Austrian's talents: he was a German emigrant, a fine yarn-spinner but this time equipped with a firm moral backbone (in fact, he is an unusually decent force in Tarantino's universe). Schultz, together with Django, would be our guide to the dark heart of Tarantino's own nation.

'I wanted to go into the bleakest time in American history,' he reported. 'Truly the biggest sin in this country. We haven't got past the sin. We can't even deal with it.'[2] It was as if he was digging to the thematic root of his own work: race, crime and the social segregation that underpinned the American Dream.

'We all intellectually "know" the brutality and inhumanity of slavery,' he said, 'but after you do the research it's no longer intellectual any more, no longer just historical record – you feel it in your bones. It makes you angry, and want to do something … I'm here to tell you, that however bad things get in the movie, a lot worse shit actually happened.'[3]

Tarantino was nearing his fiftieth birthday, and as uncompromising as he had ever been. He had come to accept that he was more an eccentric passenger of Hollywood than native. 'I still kind of feel like I'm always trying to prove I belong here,'[4] he admitted. Over the years, he had been offered high profile films like temptations to conform, scripts like *Speed* and *Men in Black*. Tellingly, he and Pierce Brosnan had concocted a plan to take James Bond back to the 1960s, remaking *Casino Royale* with a deglamorized, almost film noir vernacular. The producers fled in terror.

He was too much his own man ever to comply with Hollywood thinking. Studios were hardly queuing up to make Westerns, or slave dramas, let alone postmodern(ish)

fusions of the two. But that is exactly what he was proposing.

Once Schultz has freed Django, initially to help him identify a pair of miscreants due a bullet or two, they form a duo, crisscrossing a mud-splattered, weather-beaten, nineteenth-century America, humming with authenticity, picking off more bounties. Then Django tells his partner about his wife Broomhilda von Shaft (Kerry Washington), still out there somewhere, a slave whom he is determined to free. They discover her whereabouts: a vast plantation known as Candieland run by a silk-tongued devil named Calvin Candie. Schultz, the brains, concocts a plan to charm their way into Candie's inner sanctum and abscond with Broomhilda. Of course, according to the perverse laws of the Tarantino universe, plans are devised in order to go wrong. Only in catastrophe do characters reveal themselves.

This was to be Tarantino's most smoothly entrained narrative: no chapters, no time warping, no clever-clever asides (although there are flashbacks and some flavoursome captions) but a story told top to tail. Unlike Nazi-occupied France, he felt this particular realm of historical poison should be played straight (a relative distinction).

**Above:** Schultz (Waltz) and his partner Django (Jamie Foxx) consult the paperwork concerning their next bounty. With its untamed vision of historical vengeance – in this case tackling slavery – *Django Unchained* worked almost as a companion piece to *Inglourious Basterds*.

To a degree, *Django Unchained* can be traced back to the writing of *Inglourious Basterds*, and its yet-to-be filmed parallel story *Killer Crow*, which deals with a squad of vengeful black soldiers, alighting from prison to shoot white soldiers who had it coming (racial ethics had also been confronted in *Pulp Fiction* and *Jackie Brown*). *Killer Crow* would complete a trilogy of period vengeance pictures conceived like ultraviolent fairy tales.

'When slave narratives are done on film,' said Tarantino, 'they tend to be historical with a capital H, with an arms-length quality to them. I wanted to break that history-under-glass aspect, I wanted to throw a rock through that glass and shatter it for all times, and take you into it.'[5]

In the film's second half, having made its way to Candieland, he was going to depict the horrors of slavery with the lurid ferocity of an exploitation movie. He would draw upon visions of the era nearer to his own kneejerk sensibility, as in Richard Fleischer's *Mandingo* (wherein slaves are trained to fight one another bare knuckle), portraying, in brutal clarity, his own school of fighting mandingos, and a runaway slave set upon by Candie's vicious dogs.

These films cut closer to the truth of a time when, as Tarantino put it, 'Life is cheap. Life is dirt. Life is a buffalo nickel.'[6]

**Above:** Kerry Washington as Broomhilda, Django's wife who is enslaved on Candie's plantation. Combined with Schultz's Germanic background, the name Broomhilda hints at an almost Grimm Brothers folkloric aura where heroes strive to rescue the damsel imprisoned in the castle. This mythic style is hinted at in the classical look of the film.

**Left:** Death for hire – the whimsical, gun-toting partnership of Schultz (Christoph Waltz) and Django (Jamie Foxx) provides an echo of fellow violent professionals Vincent and Jules from *Pulp Fiction*. Django's fetching green jacket and stylish saddle can be spotted among the paraphernalia of subsequent movie *The Hateful Eight*.

He felt no obligation to what he derided as 'twenty-first century political correctness.'[7] Let the controversy come, his obligation was solely to transport a modern audience back to the antebellum South of pre-Civil War Mississippi, and confront them with the reality of that era. 'I think America is one of the only countries that has not been forced to look its past sins completely in the face,'[8] he explained. It could be said of all Tarantino's films that they reflect the truth of America through the funhouse mirror of genre. This was still, indisputably, Tarantino's first Western. Whatever the subtext, he would always deliver an entertaining film.

At heart, it is the story of a former slave who rises up and becomes a mythical Western hero. He then enters the pit of Hell (aka Mississippi) to rescue his wife from the clutches of a villain. This was classical stuff, a radical new venture for the pen of Tarantino.

You can see why he first pictured Will Smith in the titular role. Here was an opportunity to subvert and enrich the biggest black star on the planet, and he came close. They spent a number of hours together in New York where Smith was shooting *Men in Black 3* (the franchise Tarantino could have helped author). 'We went over the script and talked it out,' he recalled. 'I had a good time – he's a smart, cool guy. I think half the process was an excuse for us to hang out and spend time with one another. I had just finished the script. It was cool to talk to someone who wasn't guarded about what he was saying.'[9]

Smith confessed he had reservations about the script, especially the shudder of violence. He would be taking big risks with his image. Would his fans go with him into such dark terrain? There wasn't the time to fix the script, and Tarantino was clear he couldn't wait, and he planned to meet with Idris Elba, Chris Tucker, Terrence Howard and M.K. Williams. As the director departed, Smith turned to him and said, 'Let me just see how I feel, and if you don't find anybody, let's talk again.'[10]

'And then I found my guy,'[11] admitted Tarantino.

He knew he had his Django as soon as Jamie Foxx walked in; it was like Uma Thurman and Brad Pitt all over again – once they were in his head there was no other way to turn. Foxx had literally walked through his door, coming over to Tarantino's Hollywood Hills manse to talk it over and the director glimpsed that magical property with the actor still on the threshold. He had a 'Clint Eastwood quality.'[12]

Foxx had grown up in Texas in the 1970s. He was a high school American football star, but that didn't shield him from the racism endemic in the local culture. It had made him fiercely proud, and his pride fuelled his desire to embody the film's attack on America's repugnant soul. Indeed, on the first day of rehearsal, when it was only Waltz and Foxx, he displayed a bit too much bravado. Tarantino had to take him aside and reinforce the arc of his character.

'It was a situation where Jamie, being a strong black male wanted to be a strong black male,'[13] recalled Tarantino, throwing a light onto his confidence with actors. He explained to Foxx that they wouldn't have a story if Django was already a 'magnificent heroic character'[14]. He had to *become* that character. When we first meet him, in that chilly opening scene, he has been walking from Mississippi to Texas. He should be half dead, Tarantino insisted, nearly broken. 'He is not Jim Brown. He is not a superhero.'[15] It was genre draped in a jacket of realism.

Leonardo DiCaprio, with the sway of a heavyweight Hollywood player, had the means to get his hands on Tarantino's latest script without being on the director's list. Out of nowhere, he had expressed interest in Landa in *Inglourious Basterds*, he even offered fluent German, but not quite Waltz's ability to serve syllables like a tennis stroke. What he did present to *Django Unchained* was a honey-sweet Southern accent and a smile like a scythe. Tarantino had never established Candie's age in the script, but he had imagined him older. There had been an actor in mind, although he never revealed his identity. The problem was he had been imagining that actor from twenty years earlier. He was now too old.

In casting terms, *Django Unchained* was the least specific he had ever been. His luck deserted him. Best intentions kept falling apart, requiring hasty rewrites. He had wanted Kevin Costner for Ace Woody, but scheduling difficulties forbade that plan.

**Above:** Jamie Foxx's Django makes the acquaintance of Franco Nero's slave-owner Amerigo Vessepi. Nero, of course, played the original gun-slinging antihero in Sergio Corbucci's original *Django*, hence the in-joke about the correct pronunciation.

His next thought for Candie's right-hand man who trained the mandingo combatants was to re-team with Kurt Russell, but when the production was delayed he too had to drop out, and the character was dropped, with much of his dialogue given to Billy Crash (Walton Goggins). Sacha Baron Cohen had been cast as a character named Scotty, who loses Broomhilda to Candie in a card game, but the flashback was ditched. The reason Tarantino gives his cameo as Frankie, a mining employee with an uncertain Australian accent, was that he had cast the Australian actor Anthony LaPaglia and liked the idea of keeping his accent, another émigré in the melting pot of America. When LaPaglia dropped out as the production overran, Tarantino picked up both the role and the accent. In honour of Corbucci, Franco Nero, the star of *Django*, shares a memorable cameo with Jamie Foxx.

DiCaprio's interest in the despicable Candie was a stroke of good fortune. Although the actor was thirty-eight years old, Tarantino became excited by the idea of his villain as a boy emperor. Candieland, stretching sixty-five miles across sweltering Delta country, was its own kingdom with a hierarchy ascending from slaves to white workers, all jostling for position around their decadent ruler. 'It was just European aristocracy ad hoc,'[16] he intuited. They kept what they liked and made up a load of stuff to go along with it. And Candie, he grasped, was the 'petulant boy emperor.'[17] He thought of him as Caligula, a hedonist tired of the cotton business, indulging his violent whims. He was the first villain Tarantino had ever written than he didn't like.

The most provocative role of all would fall almost inevitably into the fearless palms of Samuel L. Jackson. Stephen was Candie's housemaster, a devious, almost

**Above:** Leonardo DiCaprio as Calvin Candie. DiCaprio was injured during shooting, when the head of the hammer he is holding flew off and struck him in the head. The prop had to be replaced with a rubber version.

**Opposite:** Alabama-born Walton Goggins as Candie henchman Billy Crash. Quentin Tarantino had spotted Goggins and his fast-talking character in the hit TV neo-Western 'Justified', and would bring his striking Southern presence back for *The Hateful Eight*.

Uncle Tom-like slave curdled into cruelty and pathetic subservience to his master. Jackson had assumed Django was being written for him. It had been three films since his friend had offered him a role of any substance. Early on, Tarantino had indeed conceptualized, then abandoned, a version of the story where following a couple of scenes revealing Django's origin story, we would leap forward to the aftermath of the Civil War (when *The Hateful Eight* will be set) and have him an older hero. As it evolved, Jackson was about fifteen years too old for the role, which he took in good part, even when he was offered vile Stephen instead.

Did he have any problem with playing the part, asked Tarantino, having sent over the script?

'Do I have a problem playing the most despicable black motherfucker in the history of the world?' he retorted. 'No, I ain't got no problem with that.'[18]

He was already working on greying up his temples and giving Stephen a distinctive limp. The character completed an elegant mirror of partnerships in the film: Schultz and Django's honourable pairing contrasting with Candie and Stephen's sour dependency.

Shooting over the final months of 2011 and into 2012, they found an exterior for Candieland at the Evergreen Plantation in Edgard, Louisiana, in the hinterlands of New Orleans. Graced with haunting cypresses and a spectacular avenue of oaks, it offered one of the best preserved plantations in the South, complete with twenty-two slave cabins. This was a landscape every bit as real as the shopping malls and bars of *Jackie Brown*'s South Bay. During their time there, Tarantino rented out a local cinema and ran Western double-bills for his cast and crew.

*Django Unchained* signalled a new era for Tarantino. Other than *Grindhouse*, this was the first time he had made a film without Lawrence Bender's calm presence at his side. There was no acrimony in the split, each was simply looking to try new things. That said, they have yet to reunite on a project and their production company A Band Apart has lain dormant. It was also the first of Tarantino's films not to be edited by the great Sally Menke. She had died suddenly from the effects of the heat when walking her dog in Griffith Park, LA.

**Right:** The perverse relationship of Candie (Leonardo DiCaprio) and his sour head slave Stephen (Samuel L. Jackson) was conceived as the sinister inversion of Schultz (Christoph Waltz) and Django (Jamie Foxx).

To portray Schultz and Django's iconographic tour of an America (as invested in movie lore as *Kill Bill Volume 1* but as rough-hewn as *Kill Bill Volume 2*), they took in locations in California and Wyoming. Throughout this journey into a 'Heart of Darkness'[19], picking off Schultz's notebook of target bounties, Django readies himself for the task ahead. Like *Inglourious Basterds*, this was a cinematic revenge fantasy redressing the sins of the past. But in this case Tarantino also wanted to address what he saw as a sin committed by cinema itself in D.W. Griffith's positive portrayal of the Klan in *The Birth of a Nation* (1915).

In a comic proto-Klan sequence, in which the riders struggle to see through their makeshift hoods, he was deliberately parodying not only Griffith but also John Ford, who had played one of those very Klansmen in the original. He wasn't a fan: in his subtextual researches he came to dislike how Ford 'kept alive this idea of Anglo-Saxon humanity.'[20]

By Django's final confrontation with Candie's posse of plantation hands, the film returns us fully to the realms of Spaghetti Westerns, with gunfights orchestrated in high style. Tarantino made sure Django's bullets did the maximum amount of bodily damage. More than even *Inglourious Basterds*, which seemed to exist in a parallel universe, Tarantino was drifting back and forth between a grim reality and thrill-seeking genre, art and riotous excess.

Some critics bought into this confluence of opposing forces. 'There is a strange and brilliant magic at work here; a dark, bubbling alchemy of art and junk,' celebrated Robbie Collin in *The Telegraph*. Philip French in *The Observer* admired Tarantino's 'adroit harnessing of the Spaghetti Western to his own aims and purposes.'

**Opposite:** Leonardo DiCaprio as Candie observes his kingdom between takes. While the character had never been written as specifically being young, Quentin Tarantino thrilled to the idea of a petulant young emperor bored of his riches.

**Above:** Dressed for the part of his cameo as a mining employee, Quentin Tarantino frames a shot. In some senses, while certainly operatic in scope, *Django Unchained* remains Tarantino's most morally empassioned film.

'Tarantino was drifting back and forth between a grim reality and thrill-seeking genre, art and riotous excess.'

But Spike Lee was on his case again, claiming his disrespect for slavery means he will never see the film. 'The horror that *Django Unchained* expresses isn't of slavery, finally,' chided Nick Pinkerton in *Sight & Sound*, 'but of a filmmaker attempting historical tragedy while shackled by his own supercilious persona.' A shot of an unarmed white woman blasted through a doorway with a shotgun was designed to evoke laughter.

In any case, the film's balance of darkness, high adventure, camp vulgarity and Tarantino's muscular language did translate into audiences. It became his biggest hit with $425 million taken worldwide. As if setting down a paragraph in a subtextual study of his work yet to be written, Tarantino made his case for why the film's contradictory forces made sense to him. 'I'm highlighting [the era] mythically and operatically, and in terms of violence and gruesomeness, with pitch-black humour. That's all part of the Spaghetti Western genre, but I'm doing it about a section of history that couldn't be more surreal, bizarre, cruel or perversely comedic when looked at from a certain view. They go hand in hand.'[21] In short, this was Quentin unchained.

Ironically, there was also some concern that, for once, his film had divided so clearly along moral lines. Unabashed goodness didn't wholly suit Tarantino. Christopher Benfey in *The New York Review of Books* expressed his disappointment that, 'No room is left for the ugly, the ambiguous, the in-between.' Not to worry, Tarantino would embrace an entire lack of moral rectitude in his next film, which would, by definition, be hateful.

# 'IT'S ALMOST AS IF I'VE NEVER MADE A PERIOD MOVIE.'

## The Hateful Eight and Once Upon a Time in Hollywood

'I'm doing it to save film,' declared Quentin Tarantino, 'and because I can.'[1] This was the justification for why he had shot his eighth film in the antique format of 70mm, which had required the Panavision camera company to dig out lenses not used since *Khartoum* in 1966.

While his friends and colleagues espoused the convenience of digital cameras, Tarantino was embracing the antediluvian approach. The past holding greater sway over his imagination than the future ever could.

He wasn't stopping there either. At his behest, The Weinstein Company (the Weinsteins having finally departed Miramax) instituted a grand roadshow presentation of his new picture where select theatres projected an extended cut of the original 70mm (true letterbox) format. 'I want to bring back some of the ballyhoo, the *showmanship*,'[2] he barked triumphantly.

As modern audiences happily streamed movies, *his* movies, on their laptops and phones, *The Hateful Eight* was an emphatic reassertion of the cinematic. The idea of films being shrunk onto screens the size of

a cigarette packet depressed him. It is no surprise to hear that he is a zealot for vinyl. He still writes his scripts by hand. 'You don't need technology for poetry,'[3] he sneered. With a touch of poetic contrariness, with the exception of the breathtaking vistas of the opening chapter, his great 70mm extravaganza was set in a single, ramshackle room. And this was another Western.

Then *The Hateful Eight* was designed to confound. Don't let the old-time setting fool you, Tarantino teased, 'I really was creating a little Agatha Christie thing.'[4]

It hadn't been an auspicious beginning. The script had been leaked onto the internet, which wasn't helpful for a story dependent on a complex chain of feints and twists. In a fit of pique, Tarantino reacted by publicly announcing that he was turning *The Hateful Eight* into a novel instead.

**Above:** Quentin Tarantino at the premiere of *The Hateful Eight* in 2015. True to his word, after twenty-five years in the business, there was no hint of compromise in his work. He had also outlasted the tides of fashion, in every sense now a classic auteur.

NO ONE COMES UP HERE WITHOUT A DAMN GOOD REASON

THE 8TH FILM BY
QUENTIN TARANTINO

THE HATEFUL EIGHT

SAMUEL L. **JACKSON** KURT **RUSSELL** JENNIFER **JASON LEIGH** WALTON **GOGGINS** DEMIAN **BICHIR** TIM **ROTH** MICHAEL **MADSEN** AND BRUCE **DERN**

THE WEINSTEIN COMPANY PRESENTS THE 8TH FILM BY QUENTIN TARANTINO "THE HATEFUL EIGHT" STARRING JAMES PARKS AND CHANNING TATUM CASTING BY VICTORIA THOMAS MUSIC BY ENNIO MORRICONE COSTUME DESIGNER COURTNEY HOFFMAN EDITOR FRED RASKIN ACE PRODUCTION DESIGNER YOHEI TANEDA DIRECTOR OF PHOTOGRAPHY ROBERT RICHARDSON ASC EXECUTIVE PRODUCER BOB WEINSTEIN HARVEY WEINSTEIN GEORGIA KACANDES PRODUCED BY RICHARD N. GLADSTEIN STACEY SHER SHANNON McINTOSH WRITTEN AND DIRECTED BY QUENTIN TARANTINO COMING SOON

**Above:** Tarantino never thought of *The Hateful Eight* as a Western per se. As far as he was concerned, the snowbound setting and assortment of suspicious strangers were the trappings of a traditional whodunit. Although what they dun wasn't entirely clear either.

Speaking to fellow director Christopher Nolan for an onstage interview at the Directors Guild of America, he explained that he had gone about this script in a different way. 'I spent time with the material, to see how I felt.'[5] He had written three drafts, pursuing each one to a different ending. He admitted that he had reacted so badly to the leak because that had only been the first draft. 'They were really kicking me in the shins over this process.'[6]

His mojo was restored having been persuaded by his friend, the film critic Elvis Mitchell, to do a live, onstage read-through of the script as part of the Los Angeles County Museum of Art's annual Live Read series. What did he have to lose? The story was available to anyone with access to Google. Moreover, not since *Reservoir Dogs* had he been working on such a theatrical footing. Then the chief inspiration for his eighth film was his first. Tarantino was coming full circle. Tim Roth would even bleed to death again from a bullet to the gut.

A clutter of unwholesome souls are holed up in a lonely cabin high in the Wyoming mountains, a venue named Minnie's Haberdashery despite it having no greater ambition than to be a hostelry on the stagecoach trail to the fictional town of Red Rock. The era is post-Civil War, but exactly how long past is left ambiguous. It could be six, eight or ten years after the conflict, but the smoke of war still lingers in the air. The reprobates at the Haberdashery split roughly along a North-South divide, most obviously in Major Marquis Warren, an ex-Union officer and former slave, and the aged General Sandford Smithers, a Confederate relic and bitter racist. The catalyst for the ensuing carnage is notorious bounty hunter John Ruth, and the captive chained to his wrist, Daisy Domergue, due to be hanged as part of a murderous gang once the snow clears.

'The film I ended up making ends up being a really serious examination of both Civil War and post-Civil War survivors,'[7] explained Tarantino. The atmosphere he sought was almost post-apocalyptic with these survivors trapped together in a freezing wasteland, blaming one another for their ruin. 'But the apocalypse is the Civil War,'[8] noted Tarantino. As well as the warehouse-bound power shifts of *Reservoir Dogs*, he was calling on the frozen paranoia of John Carpenter's The Thing, which had starred Kurt Russell. Critics also cited Eugene O'Neill's famous play, *The Iceman Cometh*, which dealt with the patrons of a

Greenwich Village saloon. Tarantino noted the influence of the self-contained television episodes of Westerns he lapped up as a kid: 'Bonanza', 'The High Chaparral' and 'The Virginian'.

*The Hateful Eight*, as the name suggests, are as irredeemably a black-hearted collection as had ever spoken up in Tarantino's imagination, and the single white female in their midst, the grinning Daisy, is the most psychotic of the bunch. She would also be the focus of prolonged battery, before being graphically hanged. Tarantino had worried that he was drifting into misogynistic territory. So the second draft was written entirely from Daisy's perspective, and he was horrified to discover that he could happily 'hang her from the highest beam.'[9]

The tension needed to be as constant as a heartbeat. Violence could erupt at any

**Above:** 1970s great Bruce Dern as Confederate relic General Sandy Smithers. Dern was another actor who brought appropriate baggage with him to the film. In this case, a history in television Westerns like 'Gunsmoke' and 'Wagon Train', many of which his director could quote verbatim on set.

moment. Again the director thought of his film as a novel, where the strictures of taste never seem to apply. 'Novels could go anywhere,' he said, 'in a way that movies aren't allowed to.'[10] It would weaken the story to treat one of the eight differently from the others because she was a woman. Tarantino was willing to admit that the first time Daisy is struck by Ruth, 'it was meant to send a shockwave through the audience.'[11]

The live reading took place at the Ace Hotel in Los Angeles on 19 April 2014, with Kurt Russell as John Ruth, the constant Samuel L. Jackson as Warren, Bruce Dern as Smithers, Michael Madsen as Joe Gage,

**Opposite:** Kurt Russell as the formidable bounty hunter John Ruth. Russell's subtle, or not so subtle, impression of John Wayne in his characterization is entirely deliberate – he even utters the line 'That'll be the day' from *The Searchers*.

a loner cowboy, Tim Roth as an itinerant English hangman named Oswaldo Mowbray (a garrulous part which suggested Christoph Waltz) and Walton Goggins as Chris Mannix, who claimed to be the newly incumbent sheriff of Red Rock. All of whom were cast in the film. Each character may or may not have a connection to Daisy, played at that point by Amber Tamblyn. The French actor Denis Ménochet played French Bob, who in the film changed nationality to Mexican in the person of Demián Bichir. Tarantino, dressed in a bandana, provided stage directions (and occasionally shushed the audience). The ebb and flow of double-

**Above:** *The Hateful Eight* was Samuel L. Jackson's sixth collaboration with Quentin Tarantino. The part of Major Marquis Warren had, of course, been written with him in mind.

**Right:** Jennifer Jason Leigh as the despicable Daisy Domergue. Leigh was another cast member who was gratified that her director always cast from an understanding of film history and not who might be currently in demand. When he looked at an actor, she said, he knew their entire career.

crosses, unexpected alliances and outbreaks of gunfire proved thrilling.

So Tarantino thought better of his decision, and completed a third draft, revising the ending. Shooting began on the 900-acre Schmid Ranch in Telluride, Colorado in December 2014, not so far from the Sundance Labs where Tarantino had once been advised to avoid long, talky scenes.

At one point he had conceived *The Hateful Eight* as a direct sequel to *Django Unchained* called *Django in White Hell*.

But the mystery was undermined if we had a hero. Still, this remains the same Tarantino-universe (with Jackson and Goggins playing different characters): when we meet Jackson's Warren in the blizzard he is seated on Django's distinctive saddle, and the gunfighter's green corduroy jacket can be spotted in the Haberdashery. The punctilious Oswaldo is thought to be a forebear of Michael Fassbender's Archie Hicox in *Inglourious Basterds*.

Given he was seeking a cadence of *Reservoir Dogs*, Tarantino wanted 'cool

nineties actors'[12] but grown older, hence Roth and Madsen, while the splendid Russell with a monstrous moustache offered a seasoned version of his gnarly 1980s personae as Snake Plissken or R.J. MacReady from *The Thing*. Quite deliberately, Tarantino had avoided casting a big star. This needed to be an ensemble where it was impossible to decipher a natural hierarchy among the actors. While Channing Tatum's name on the poster hinted that the plot might not be limited to an octet of hateful persons.

Jennifer Jason Leigh was younger than Tarantino had in mind for Daisy. But he couldn't forget the 'bloodcurdling scream'[13] she gave in the audition. If that had been in someone's house, he thought, they would have called the cops. He had narrowed it down to three actresses, who had 'all made their bones in the nineties.'[14] He put on personal film festivals of the three, 'and, frankly, it was the Jennifer Jason Leigh festival that I enjoyed the most.'[15]

*Single White Female*, *Mrs. Parker and the Vicious Circle*, *Miami Blues*, *The Hitcher*: 'She was like a female Sean Penn,'[16] he gushed. Beneath her loopy-loo bluster, Leigh subtly conveys a scheming mind (Daisy is the deceiver in the midst as Mr. Orange once was) as the plot knuckles down into uncovering who in the Haberdashery might be part of her gang.

As with the live read, Tarantino provides the brief steers of narration like the voice of God, the storyteller almighty.

They shot the splendid exteriors in Colorado under trying conditions, the vital snowfall refusing to cooperate. The one-piece, almost Tardis-like expanse of the Haberdashery interior was more manageable as a set in LA, which the director kept refrigerated so that the actors' breath steamed authentically as they spoke and

coffee, even poisoned coffee, sent up misty zephyrs into the moody lamplight.

Shooting in 70mm might seem counterintuitive for such an interior film, but there was method in Tarantino's widescreen madness. 'I didn't treat anything differently,' he claimed to Nolan. 'I did what I needed to do.'[17] With so much information in the frame there was no need to embellish. And the wide frame brought with it an intimacy.

'I've shot a lot of close-ups of Sam Jackson, but I've never shot them as I did in

this movie,' he boasted. 'You find yourself taking backstrokes in his eyes.'[18]

The format put you inside the space. Up close. Every frame operates on dual levels: the foreground action, bursting with prime, vituperative Tarantino dialogue; and then what the characters are up to the background. A second viewing reveals layers within every scene.

There was something about the integrity of the material that demanded a score. He approached Ennio Morricone who, quite

apart from his Spaghetti Western themes, had provided plangent accompaniment for *The Thing*. 'You are my favourite composer,' Tarantino told him. 'And I need the score in a month.'[19]

Understandably, the eighty-seven-year-old Morricone turned him down. Then he read the script, and a theme came straightaway to the maestro: a rumbling accompaniment for the travelling stagecoach charged with incipient violence. He informed Tarantino he would do the

main themes. In fact, fittingly, there are a few unused pieces from *The Thing*, but this is seventy per cent an original score, eschewing the skyward operatics of the Western for a swampy, 1960s-style thriller groove filled with lurking dread.

What Tarantino especially loved about Westerns, was how they took the temperature of their times. Back in the 1950s, they were lit with the sunburst optimism of the Eisenhower era. In the 1970s, they became revisionist, these postmodern Watergate

Westerns steeped in paranoia. In the 1980s, films like Silverado carried the rah-rah sentiment of the Reagan administration. 'You have to do your version of a Western,'[20] he maintained, one that was inevitably a corollary of the second decade of the twenty-first century.

Minnie's Haberdashery is a microcosm of America, burning with hatred – much of it racial. The film had been written in the wake of the Baltimore and Ferguson shootings of unarmed black men by police, and Tarantino was investigating the roots of the violence on his television screen. 'Finally, the issue of white supremacy is being talked about and dealt with,' he acknowledged. 'And that is what the movie is about.'[21]

Tarantino was in a political mood. He had openly supported Barack Obama and attended an anti-police Black Lives Matter rally in New York City in the build up to the film's release. 'I'm here to say I'm on the side of the murdered,'[22] he announced, addressing the rally. In retaliation, the police union called for a boycott of the film. Tarantino admitted they had lost valuable commercial tie-ins as a result.

The film did a respectable $156 million worldwide, but it was framed as a failure compared to his recent smash hits. Tarantino tried to shrug it off. 'My name is not a carton of milk that has an expiration date,'[23] he smarted.

*The Hateful Eight* may have run the gamut with critics on release ('A nasty prank foisted on willing suckers,' grumbled Stuart Klawans in *The Nation*; a 'thriller percolating with close-quarters paranoia

and Hawksian gab,' sang Joshua Rothkopf in *Time Out*) but it now stands tall among his work: intense, riveting, both nasty and funny (often simultaneously), provocative, and so accomplished. As Tarantino himself proclaimed, 'It's going to be available twenty years, thirty years, hopefully one hundred years from now.'[24]

Where would his muse venture next? The answer was literally to Hollywood. But this was a Hollywood born in the mind of Quentin Tarantino, a vivid and brilliant fusion of life and art, and his most personal film.

He has admitted that those oft-mentioned prequels and sequels – *The Vega Brothers*, *Killer Crow*, *Django/Zorro* – looked less interesting with time, although he hasn't ruled out *Kill Bill: Volume 3*. If he had anything left to prove, it was only to himself. And on 11 July 2017, following two years of quiet and twenty-five years since *Reservoir Dogs*, he began shooting *Once Upon a Time in Hollywood*, which would intermingle fictional and real events, chiefly the crimes orchestrated by cult leader Charles Manson.

Tarantino's fascination with Manson can be traced back to the first stirrings of *Natural Born Killers*, which found its inspiration in the quasi-deification of a psychopath by the media. On the steps of the courthouse where the film's serial killer lovers are standing trial, a grinning fan notes that Mickey and Mallory's killing spree is 'the best thing to happen to mass murder since Manson.'[25] Promoting *The Hateful Eight*, Tarantino liked to describe Daisy as 'a Manson girl out West.'[26]

Manson, his followers and most famous victim, the actress Sharon Tate, will be the first historical figures in the Tarantino oeuvre, leaving aside the cartoon cameos of Churchill, Hitler and assorted cronies in *Inglourious Basterds*.

Tarantino was only seven when members of the Manson Family broke into Tate's home on Cielo Drive to murder the pregnant actress, but he has a clear memory of the time. In fact, the entire story is retrofitted through the lens of his memories: all the sights, sounds and idiosyncrasies of a Los Angeles caught in the hinterland between

# 'Promoting The Hateful Eight, Tarantino liked to describe Daisy as 'a Manson girl out West.'

**Above:** For his ninth film, Tarantino is injecting a wide-ranging Los Angeles crime story with the real-life murder of actress Sharon Tate orchestrated by cult leader Charles Manson. A fascination with the events of summer 1969 can be traced all the way back to *Natural Born Killers*.

the 1960s and 1970s. This is not the 1969 of historical record; this is *Once Upon a Time in Hollywood*, a fairy tale, and, with its titular nod to Sergio Leone, a Spaghetti Western.

So, we get a very Tarantinoesque thread in which we catch up with fictional television actor Rick Dalton following the cancellation of his 'Bonanza'-style Western serial, 'Bounty Law'. His plan is to follow Clint Eastwood into the Spaghetti Western business, accompanied by his faithful stunt double. Each in their second Tarantino film, Leonardo DiCaprio is the ersatz gunslinger with Brad Pitt as his stuntman cum factotum Cliff Booth. *Death Proof*, with its insider jokes and twisted stunt man, is a calling card for *Once Upon a Time in Hollywood*.

Tarantino explained, 'Rick's kind of working his way down the ladder – and

Cliff's working his way down the ladder too.'[27] In this fictive branch of Hollywood history, Dalton happens to live next door to Tate. Booth, meanwhile, lives in a trailer (like Budd in *Kill Bill: Volume 2*) stationed opposite a drive-in cinema.

This was the closest thing Tarantino had ever done to *Pulp Fiction*. 'It takes place in Los Angeles,' he mused, 'and there's three stories going on simultaneously: there's Sharon's story, there's Rick's story, and there's Cliff's story. It's a whole cast of characters like there is in *Pulp Fiction*, and it takes place over a course of a couple of days, just like *Pulp Fiction* does.'[28]

One particular strand of enquiry into Hollywood lore, finds Rick's celebrity wilting beneath the stardom of Steve McQueen (Damien Lewis). Old-school Dalton also

**Above:** Leonardo DiCaprio, as Western star Rick Dalton, confers with Tarantino on set of the set within the set. As its title implies, *Once Upon a Time in Hollywood* marks the first time the director has explored the world of filmmaking within one of this scripts.

finds himself confounded by a studio system embracing the sophistications of European cinema. The period is not only significant for the Manson murders; the Golden Era of Hollywood was in its death throes. Giving the 2016 Lyon Film Festival master class – entitled '1970' – he cited Mark Harris' *Scenes From a Revolution* as an inspiration. Harris' book surveys the making of the five Best Picture nominees of 1967, which pitched New Hollywood trailblazers *The Graduate* and *Bonnie and Clyde* against middlebrow

**Left:** Margot Robbie as Sharon Tate, in real-life the actress murdered by members of Charles Manson's cult, better known as the 'Family'. While we have had comically exaggerated versions of Hitler and Churchill in *Inglorious Basterds*, this is the first true intersection of Tarantino's movie universe with historical events.

Archives. Film history was on his mind. You wonder whether Rick's confusion is a mask for the director's concerns that he is now a bygone spirit amid the blast of modern Hollywood.

Habitually, the concept was first tested as a novel written during *Django Unchained*. In stark contrast to the tightly framed crooks of *The Hateful Eight*, as it evolved into a script that took five years to complete, Tarantino found room for over 100 different speaking parts, blurring the lines between fact, fiction and the tapestry of his previous films.

As Tate, the 26-year-old actress wife of then feted Polish director Roman Polanski (played by Polish actor Rafał Zawierucha), Tarantino only ever had Australian star Margot Robbie in mind, beforehand making sure he gained the approval of Deborah Tate, the victim's sister. Al Pacino, new to the jive of Tarantino's universe, portrays Dalton's loquacious agent Marvin Shwarz, who recalls publicist and producer Marvin Schwarz, responsible for the 1969 Burt Reynolds Western *100 Rifles*. Dakota Fanning is prominent Manson acolyte Lynette 'Squeaky' Fromme, Lena Dunham is fellow Family member Catherine Share, with Australian actor Damon Herriman a match for the despicable guru.

social issue films such as *In the Heat of the Night* and *Guess Who's Coming to Dinner* and the populist nonsense of *Doctor Doolittle*. 'It was increasingly clear that something was dying,' claimed Harris, 'and something was being created.'[29]

This was Tarantino on Hollywood's transitional period. Actors, directors, producers, agents, stunt men, models and madmen: the whole movie scene taking over from his usual assortment of molls and hitmen. 'New Hollywood had won by the end of 1967, only they didn't know it yet,' explained Tarantino to the gathered cineastes. 'And old Hollywood was over by the end 1967 even though they didn't know it yet… By 1970 New Hollywood had won.'[30] Significantly, this was when Tarantino consciously experienced cinema for the first time. His transitional period, if you like.

In 2014, Tarantino took over programming duties at the New Beverly Cinema, explicitly running it as a revival house like a new incarnation of Video

**Left:** Brad Pitt as laid-back stunt man Cliff Booth. While both his career and his life are intimately tied to the fate of Dalton, Booth will have a strand of the entwined story all his own. Akin to the playfulness of the *Kill Bill* films, *Once upon a Time in Hollywood* ponders the difference between fake 'movie violence' and 'real violence'.

**Top:** Rick Dalton (DiCaprio) makes an appearance on pop television show *Hullabaloo*, a real magazine show featured all the music trends of the moment, which ran from 1965-66. Naturally, Tarantino was an avid fan.

**Above:** Sharon Tate (Robbie) takes a stroll along Tarantino's hometown streets (with regular cinematographer Robert Richardson operating the camera). Recreating the look and feel 1960s Los Angeles to the director's exact specification made this technically the hardest film he has ever had to make.

The late Luke Perry is Scott Lancer, a 'real' character from real 'Bonanza' clone 'Lancer'. Whereas Scoot McNairy plays Business Bob Gilbert, a fictional character from the made-up show 'Bounty Law'. There was also room for Emile Hirsch, Timothy Olyphant, James Marsden and Tarantino regulars Roth and Russell.

Adding to this dizzying meta-blend of personnel, was martial artist Mike Moh as Bruce Lee, the star whose iconic canary yellow jump suit was borrowed by The Bride for *Kill Bill: Volume 1*. Also involved was Maya Hawke, daughter of *Kill Bill*'s Uma Thurman, as a flower girl, and Rumer Willis, daughter of *Pulp Fiction*'s Bruce Willis, as Joanna Pettet, who lunched with Tate hours before she was murdered.

Shooting for four months through the summer of 2017 (twenty years since he was on the streets with *Jackie Brown*), the director may have traversed the city that has been his base and inspiration, but he deliberately moved out of home for the duration. It was a psychological thing – establishing the mind set that you are on location. All other considerations in life were set aside for filmmaking.

Having severed ties with The Weinstein Company, caught in the throes of a much documented scandal and bankruptcy, Tarantino formed an unexpected alliance with British producer David Heyman (the man behind the *Harry Potter* and *Paddington* films). Before a frame of film was shot, Heyman marshalled a bake-off among the major studios for the right to back a $98 million Hollywood satire. What would the young Tarantino, having his scripts returned by appalled studio readers, think of his older self being flanked by CEOs clamouring for the honour of his next film? It came down to Warner Bros.,

Paramount and Sony Pictures. Warner Bros. decked their boardroom in 1960s decor, but Tarantino chose Sony, banking on the marketing nous that took the international box office of *Django Unchained*, a Western about slavery, to over $250 million.

'This is easily the hardest movie I've ever made,' he confessed mid-shoot, 'because 1969 is so different to 2018. It's almost as if I've never made a period movie before.'[31] A challenge made no easier when Burt Reynolds suffered a fatal heart attack before shooting a scene as George Spahn, the (real) former silent Western star who turns a literal blind eye on the Manson Family holing up at his ranch. Bruce Dern was hastily corralled as a replacement.

An entire era needed to be fashioned anew. Los Angeles had changed beyond recognition since the turbulent days of 1969 – even those neglected boroughs that are the director's preferred haunts. Right across the film, Tarantino pursued a level of pictorial detail that would go above the heads of even the old gang at Video Archives.

The result is a fabulous exercise in time travel. Every billboard advertises the exact films that were playing at that time. The Spahn Ranch, lair of the Manson Family and former backdrop to 'Bonanza', was meticulously rebuilt at the Corrigan Ranch in California's Simi Valley. And they turned back the clock at the El Coyote Café, on Beverly Boulevard, where Tate and her inner circle enjoyed their last meal.

More than Tarantino's instinct for cult cinema, his ninth film teems with references to that steady diet of television that occupied his idle youth (and bled into *The Hateful Eight*). Coincidentally, or not, Manson was reputed to be a big devotee of television Westerns. Rick's recently cancelled 'Bounty Law' might be fictional, but we learn he has

**Above:** DiCaprio's television star leaps into action. The character of Rick Dalton presented an ironic challenge for DiCaprio as he was asked to accurately portray an actor who hasn't quite got the talent to become a superstar as big as DiCaprio.

also guest starred in real shows like 'Lancer', 'FBI' and 'The Green Hornet'. This is a cocktail of cults and cult television.

You wonder if Tarantino's thoughts have wandered to the possibilities and budgets offered by modern television. He has not ruled out trying the small screen for size once his ten films are complete.

Meanwhile, development has continued on a new *Star Trek* movie based on an idea Tarantino pitched to series producer J.J. Abrams. When it came to science fiction, Tarantino insists he was a *Star Trek* man. Details remain sketchy but the assumption is that it will involve the current crew: Chris Pine as Kirk, Zachary Quinto as Spock and Simon Pegg as Scotty. Remarkably, it was confirmed that it will be R-rated, with phasers set to kill. Given Abrams has set up a writing room on the project that would suggest it is unlikely Tarantino will direct.

Tarantino, at fifty-five, is a middle-aged man and a survivor. So synonymous is he with a time and place, the seismic impact he made as a young man who changed the complexion of cinema, he could easily have disappeared, the flavour of the moment gone stale. Whether it is that monumental self-belief, or the insistence of that God-given talent, combined with a skilful management of his own celebrity (and bankability), the next film from Quentin Tarantino remains an event still able to stop Hollywood in its tracks, with the possibility there is only one more to come:

'If I have a change of heart, if I come up with a new story, I could come back,' he allowed. 'But if I stop at ten, that would be okay as an artistic statement.'[32]

There came a pause, an evaluation of his calling, and of a future chapter still to be written (and maybe reshuffled into the past). 'We'll see what happens. I do like the idea of leaving the audience wanting a little more.'[33]

# '...the next film from Quentin Tarantino remains an event still able to stop Hollywood in its tracks.'

# Sources

**Introduction**

**1** *Film Comment*, Gavin Smith, August 1994.
**2** *Pulp Fiction Original Screenplay*, Quentin Tarantino, Faber & Faber, 1994.

'I didn't go to film school, I went to films.'
**Video Archives**

**1** *Quentin Tarantino: The Cinema of Cool*, Jeff Dawson, Applause, 1995.
**2** *True Romance* press conference, Los Angeles, August 1993.
**3** *Quentin Tarantino: The Cinema of Cool*, Jeff Dawson, Applause, 1995.
**4** *Quentin Tarantino: The Man and His Movies,* Jami Bernard, Harper Perennial, 1995.
**5** *Quentin Tarantino: The Cinema of Cool*, Jeff Dawson, Applause, 1995.
**6** *Fresh Air with Terry Gross* (transcript), Terry Gross, 27 August 2009.
**7** Ibid.
**8** Ibid.
**9** *Positif*, Michel Ciment and Hubert Niogret, September 1992.
**10** Ibid.
**11** *Quentin Tarantino: The Cinema of Cool*, Jeff Dawson, Applause, 1995.
**12** *Fresh Air with Terry Gross* (radio transcript), Terry Gross, 27 August 2009.
**13** Ibid.
**14** *TheFilmStage.com*, Kristen Coates, 26 June 2010.
**15** *Positif*, Michel Ciment and Hubert Niogret, September 1992.
**16** *Quentin Tarantino: The Man and His Movies*, Jami Bernard, Harper Perennial, 1995.
**17** *Down and Dirty Pictures*, Peter Biskind, Simon & Schuster, 2004.
**18** Ibid.
**19** Ibid.
**20** Ibid.
**21** *Positif*, Michel Ciment and Hubert Niogret, September 1992.
**22** *Quentin Tarantino: The Cinema of Cool*, Jeff Dawson, Applause, 1995.
**23** *Down and Dirty Pictures*, Peter Biskind, Simon & Schuster, 2004.
**24** Ibid.
**25** *Quentin Tarantino: The Cinema of Cool*, Jeff Dawson, Applause, 1995.

'I made this movie for myself, and everyone is invited.'
**Reservoir Dogs**

**1** *Quentin Tarantino: The Cinema of Cool*, Jeff Dawson, Applause, 1995.
**2** *Quentin Tarantino: The Man and His Movies*, Jami Bernard, Harper Perennial, 1995.
**3** *Quentin Tarantino: The Cinema of Cool*, Jeff Dawson, Applause, 1995.
**4** Ibid.
**5** Ibid.
**6** *Quentin Tarantino: The Man and His Movies*, Jami Bernard, Harper Perennial, 1995.
**7** *Reservoir Dogs Original Screenplay*, Quentin Tarantino, Faber & Faber Classics, 2000.
**8** *Quentin Tarantino: The Man and His Movies*, Jami Bernard, Harper Perennial, 1995.
**9** *Reservoir Dogs Original Screenplay*, Quentin Tarantino, Faber & Faber Classics, 2000.
**10** *Positif*, Michel Ciment and Hubert Niogret, September 1992.
**11** Ibid.
**12** *Quentin Tarantino: The Cinema of Cool*, Jeff Dawson, Applause, 1995.
**13** *Quentin Tarantino: The Man and His Movies*, Jami Bernard, Harper Perennial, 1995.
**14** *Reservoir Dogs* press conference, Toronto Film Festival, 1992.
**15** *Film Comment*, Gavin Smith, August 1994.
**16** *Reservoir Dogs* press conference, Toronto Film Festival, 1992.
**17** *Down and Dirty Pictures*, Peter Biskind, Simon & Schuster, 2004.
**18** *Quentin Tarantino: The Man and His Movies*, Jami Bernard, Harper Perennial, 1995.
**19** *LA Weekly*, Ella Taylor, 16 October 1992.
**20** Ibid.
**21** Ibid.
**22** Ibid.
**23** *Down and Dirty Pictures*, Peter Biskind, Simon & Schuster, 2004.
**24** *Reservoir Dogs* press conference, Toronto Film Festival, 1992.
**25** *Down and Dirty Pictures*, Peter Biskind, Simon & Schuster, 2004.
**26** *Kaleidoscope* BBC Radio 4, Quentin Tarantino, 1995.
**27** *Empire*, Jeff Dawson, November 1994.

'I think of them as like old girlfriends…'
**True Romance, Natural Born Killers and From Dusk Till Dawn**

1  *True Romance* press conference, Los Angeles, August 1993.
2  *Projections 3*, Graham Fuller, Faber & Faber, 1994.
3  *True Romance Original Screenplay*, Quentin Tarantino, Grove Press, 1995.
4  *Quentin Tarantino: The Man and His Movies*, Jami Bernard, Harper Perennial, 1995.
5  Ibid.
6  *Quentin Tarantino: The Cinema of Cool*, Jeff Dawson, Applause, 1995.
7  *Projections 3*, Graham Fuller, Faber & Faber, 1994.
8  *Film Comment*, Gavin Smith, August 1994.
9  *True Romance Original Screenplay*, Quentin Tarantino, Grove Press, 1995.
10  Ibid.
11  *Quentin Tarantino: The Man and His Movies*, Jami Bernard, Harper Perennial, 1995.
12  *Quentin Tarantino: The Cinema of Cool*, Jeff Dawson, Applause, 1995.
13  *Premiere*, Peter Biskind, November 1994.
14  *Quentin Tarantino: The Man and His Movies*, Jami Bernard, Harper Perennial, 1995.
15  Ibid.
16  *Natural Born Killers Original Screenplay*, Quentin Tarantino, Grove Press, 2000.
17  *Quentin Tarantino: The Man and His Movies*, Jami Bernard, Harper Perennial, 1995.
18  Ibid.
19  *Axcess 4* No.1, Don Gibalevich, February-March 1996.
20  *Cinefantastique*, Michael Beeler, January 1996.
21  *US*, J. Hoberman, January 1996.
22  *Axcess 4* No.1, Don Gibalevich, February-March 1996.
23  *Details*, Mim Udovitch, February 1996.
24  *US*, J. Hoberman, January 1996.
25  Ibid.
26  Ibid.
27  Ibid.
28  *Inglourious Basterds Original Screenplay*, Quentin Tarantino, Little Brown, 2009.
29  *Details*, Mim Udovitch, February 1996.

'My characters never stop telling stories…'
**Pulp Fiction**

1  *Projections 3*, Graham Fuller, Faber & Faber, 1994.
2  *Sight & Sound*, Manhola Dargis, May 1994.
3  *Projections 3*, Graham Fuller, Faber & Faber, 1994.

4  *Sight & Sound*, Manhola Dargis, May 1994.
5  *Pulp Fiction Original Screenplay*, Quentin Tarantino, Faber & Faber, 1994.
6  *Down and Dirty Pictures*, Peter Biskind, Simon & Schuster, 2004.
7  *The New Yorker*, Larissa MacFarquhar, 20 October 2005.
8  *Pulp Fiction Original Screenplay*, Quentin Tarantino, Faber & Faber, 1994.
9  *Positif*, Michel Ciment and Hubert Niogret, November 1994.
10  *Quentin Tarantino: The Man and His Movies*, Jami Bernard, Harper Perennial, 1995.
11  *Down and Dirty Pictures*, Peter Biskind, Simon & Schuster, 2004.
12  *The New Yorker*, Martin Amis, 1995.
13  Ibid.
14  *Sight & Sound*, Manhola Dargis, May 1994.
15  *Quentin Tarantino: The Man and His Movies*, Jami Bernard, Harper Perennial, 1995.
16  Ibid.
17  *Magazine*, Sean O'Hagan, May 1994.
18  *Quentin Tarantino: The Man and His Movies*, Jami Bernard, Harper Perennial, 1995.
19  *Positif*, Michel Ciment and Hubert Niogret, November 1994.
20  Ibid.
21  *Quentin Tarantino: The Man and His Movies*, Jami Bernard, Harper Perennial, 1995.
22  *The Times*, Sean O'Hagan, 15 October 1994.
23  *Positif*, Michel Ciment and Hubert Niogret, November 1994.
24  *Down and Dirty Pictures*, Peter Biskind, Simon & Schuster, 2004.
25  *Quentin Tarantino: The Man and His Movies*, Jami Bernard, Harper Perennial, 1995.
26  Ibid.
27  Ibid.
28  *Down and Dirty Pictures*, Peter Biskind, Simon & Schuster, 2004.
29  Ibid.
30  *Oscar* broadcast, 27 March 1995.

'It just kind of snuck up on me.'
**Four Rooms and Jackie Brown**

1  *Time Out*, Tom Charity, 25 March 1998.
2  Ibid.
3  *The Guardian*, Simon Hattenstone, 27 February 1998.
4  *Premiere*, Peter Biskind, November 1995.
5  *Quentin Tarantino: The Man and His Movies*, Jami Bernard, Harper Perennial, 1995.
6  *Premiere*, Peter Biskind, November 1995.
7  Ibid.
8  *Quentin Tarantino: The Man and His Movies*, Jami Bernard, Harper Perennial, 1995.
9  Ibid.

**10** *Premiere*, Peter Biskind, November 1995.

**11** *Quentin Tarantino: The Man and His Movies*, Jami Bernard, Harper Perennial, 1995.

**12** Ibid.

**13** *US*, J. Hoberman, January 1996.

**14** Ibid.

**15** *Jackie Brown* press conference, Los Angeles, December 1997.

**16** *Projections 3*, Graham Fuller, Faber & Faber, 1994.

**17** *Time Out*, Tom Charity, March 25, 1998

**18** *The Chicago Sun Times*, Roger Ebert, 21 December 1997.

**19** *Jackie Brown* press conference, Los Angeles, December 1997.

**20** *The Guardian*, Adrian Wootton, 5 January 1998.

**21** *IGN*, Jeff Otto, 10 October 2003.

**22** Ibid.

**23** *Time Out*, Tom Charity, 25 March 1998.

**24** Ibid.

**25** *Jackie Brown* press conference, Los Angeles, December 1997.

**26** Ibid.

**27** *The Guardian*, Simon Hattenstone, 27 February 1998.

**28** *Jackie Brown* press conference, Los Angeles, December 1997.

**29** *The Guardian*, Adrian Wootton, 5 January 1998.

**30** Ibid.

**31** *The New Yorker*, Larissa MacFarquhar, 20 October 2005.

**32** Ibid.

**33** *The Guardian*, Simon Hattenstone, 27 February 1998.

**34** *Time Out*, Tom Charity, 25 March 1998.

### 'I don't really consider myself an American filmmaker…'
#### Kill Bill: Volumes 1 and 2

**1** *IGN*, Jeff Otto, 10 October 2003.

**2** *BBC Films*, Michaela Latham, October 2003.

**3** Ibid.

**4** Ibid.

**5** *Entertainment Weekly*, Mary Kaye Schilling, 9 April 2004.

**6** *Esquire Online*, Matt Miller, 21 January 2016.

**7** *Kill Bill Original Screenplay*, Quentin Tarantino, Fourth Estate 1989.

**8** *Screencrave*, Mali Elfman, 25 August 2009.

**9** *Eiga Hi-Ho Magazine*, Tomohiro Machiyama, 2003.

**10** *IGN*, Jeff Otto, 10 October 2003.

**11** Ibid.

**12** *Eiga Hi-Ho Magazine*, Tomohiro Machiyama, 2003.

**13** Ibid.

**14** *Screenwriters Monthly*, Fred Topel, February 2007.

**15** *Village Voice*, R.J. Smith, 1 October 2003.

**16** *The Making of Kill Bill* documentary, Uma Thurman, DVD.

**17** *IGN*, Jeff Otto, 10 October 2003.

**18** *Village Voice*, R.J. Smith, 1 October 2003.

**19** Ibid.

**20** *Eiga Hi-Ho Magazine*, Tomohiro Machiyama, 2003.

**21** *Screenwriters Monthly*, Fred Topel, February 2007.

**22** *IGN*, Jeff Otto, 10 October 2003.

**23** Ibid.

**24** *Screenwriters Monthly*, Fred Topel, February 2007.

**25** *Eiga Hi-H Magazine*, Tomohiro Machiyama, 2003.

**26** *Entertainment Weekly*, Mary Kaye Schilling, 9 April 2004.

**27** Ibid.

**28** *Kill Bill Original Screenplay*, Quentin Tarantino, Fourth Estate 1989.

### 'Slasher movies are legitimate…'
#### Grindhouse

**1** *Charlie Rose Show*, PBS, 4 May 2007.

**2** Ibid.

**3** Ibid.

**4** *Entertainment Weekly*, Chris Nashawaty, 23 June 2006.

**5** *Charlie Rose Show*, PBS, 4 May 2007.

**6** Ibid.

**7** *The Quentin Tarantino Archives*, Sebastian Haselbeck, 22 December 2008.

**8** *Sight & Sound*, Nick James, February 2008.

**9** *Charlie Rose Show*, PBS, 4 May 2007.

**10** *Sight & Sound*, Nick James, February 2008.

**11** *The Quentin Tarantino Archives*, Sebastian Haselbeck, 22 December 2008.

**12** *Sight & Sound*, Nick James, February 2008.

**13** *Charlie Rose Show*, PBS, 4 May 2007.

**14** *Sight & Sound*, Nick James, February 2008.

**15** Ibid.

**16** *The Quentin Tarantino Archives*, Sebastian Haselbeck, 22 December 2008,

**17** *IndieLondon*, uncredited, September 2008.

**18** *Sight & Sound*, Nick James, February 2008.

**19** *Vulture*, Amanda Demme, 23 August 2015.

**20** *The Hollywood Reporter* roundtable discussion, Stephen Galloway, 28 November 2012.

**21** Ibid.

**22** Ibid.

### 'Just fucking kill him.'
#### Inglourious Basterds

**1** *Screenwriters Monthly*, Fred Topel, February 2007.

**2** *Village Voice*, Ella Taylor, 18 August 2009.

**3** Ibid.

**4** *Charlie Rose Show*, PBS, 21 August 2009.

**5** Ibid.

**6** *Village Voice*, Ella Taylor, 18 August 2009.

**7** Ibid.

**8** *Inglourious Basterds*, Cannes press conference, May 2007.

**9** *The Guardian*, Sean O'Hagan, 9 August 2009.

**10** *Playboy*, Michael Fleming, 3 December 2012.

**11** Ibid.

**12** Ibid.

**13** *Village Voice*, Ella Taylor, 18 August 2009.

**14** *Screencrave*, Mali Elfman, 25 August 2009.

**15** *Inglourious Basterds Original Screenplay*, Quentin Tarantino, Little Brown, 2009.

**16** *Time Out*, Tom Huddleston, July 2009.

**17** *Inglourious Basterds*, Cannes press conference, May 2007.

**18** *Time Out*, Tom Huddleston, July 2009.

**19** Ibid.

'Life is cheap. Life is dirt. Life is a buffalo nickel.'
### Django Unchained

**1** *Charlie Rose Show*, PBS, 21 December 2012.

**2** Ibid.

**3** BAFTA Q&A, 6 December 2012.

**4** *Playboy*, Michael Fleming, 3 December 2012.

**5** BAFTA Q&A, 6 December 2012.

**6** *The Root*, Henry Louis Gates Jr., 23-25 December 2012.

**7** AALBC.com, Kam Williams, December 2012.

**8** *The Root*, Henry Louis Gates Jr., 23-25 December 2012.

**9** *Playboy*, Michael Fleming, 3 December 2012.

**10** *The Root*, Henry Louis Gates Jr., 23-25 December 2012.

**11** Ibid.

**12** *Playboy*, Michael Fleming, 3 December 2012.

**13** Ibid.

**14** Ibid.

**15** *The Root*, Henry Louis Gates Jr., 23-25 December 2012.

**16** BAFTA Q&A, 6 December 2012.

**17** *The Root*, Henry Louis Gates Jr., 23-25 December 2012.

**18** Ibid.

**19** BAFTA Q&A, 6 December 2012.

**20** *IndieWire*, Matt Singer, 27 December 2012.

**21** *Playboy*, Michael Fleming, 3 December 2012.

'It's almost as if I've never made a period movie.'
### The Hateful Eight and Once Upon a Time in Hollywood

**1** AXS TV, Dan Rather, 24 November 2015.

**2** Ibid.

**3** *Vulture*, Amanda Demme, 23 August 2015.

**4** *Entertainment Weekly*, Jeff Labrecque, 31 December 2015.

**5** Directors Guild of America Q&A, Christopher Nolan, 29 December 2015.

**6** Ibid.

**7** *Entertainment Weekly*, Jessica Derschowitz, 4 January 2016.

**8** Ibid.

**9** Directors Guild of America Q&A, Christopher Nolan, 29 December 2015.

**10** Ibid.

**11** Ibid.

**12** *Vulture*, Amanda Demme, 23 August 2015.

**13** Ibid.

**14** *Entertainment Weekly*, Jeff Labrecque, 31 December 2015.

**15** Ibid.

**16** Ibid.

**17** AXS TV, Dan Rather, 24 November 2015.

**18** *Collider*, Christina Raddish, 23 December 2015.

**19** *The Telegraph*, uncredited, 11 December 2015.

**20** Directors Guild of America Q&A, Christopher Nolan, 29 December 2015.

**21** *New York Magazine*, Lane Brown, 23 August 2015.

**22** Rally against police brutality, New York, 26 October 2015.

**23** *Entertainment Weekly*, Jeff Labrecque, 31 December 2015.

**24** Ibid.

**25** *Natural Born Killers Original Screenplay*, Quentin Tarantino, Grove Press, 2000.

**26** *USA Today*, Brian Truitt, December 25, 2015

**27** *Total Film*, Damon Wise, July 2019

**28** Ibid.

**29** *Scenes From a Revolution*, Mark Harris, 2009

**30** Lyon Film Festival Q&A, October 12, 2016

**31** *Total Film*, Damon Wise, July 2019

**32** *Playboy*, Michael Fleming, 3 December 2012.

**33** American Film Market Q&A, Mike Fleming, 20 November 2014.

### ACKNOWLEDGEMENTS

There is nowhere else to start but with Quentin Tarantino himself. In my lifetime no single director has had such a seismic impact as a writer as this livewire Californian. In person, he is everything you wish him to be: a brilliant, opinionated, erudite chatterbox. On screen, though, is where it made sense – creating a new, thrilling film experience from the body parts of old ones. As the introduction attests, to this day I have never experienced a screening like that first showing of *Pulp Fiction* in London. QT blew our brains in the early nineties, and we can only come back for more.

No auteur is anything without the great team behind him, so my heartfelt thanks go out Julia Shone, the unflappable Sue Pressley, and the perspicacious dedication of Philip de Ste Croix. Finally, my gratitude is extended to all my friends, cronies and 'archivists' who have contributed so much over the years: Damon Wise, Ian Freer, Nick de Semlyen, Mark Salisbury, Mark Dinning, and Dan Jolin. And, of course, my eternal gratitude goes to the grooviest chick of them all, Kat, who still reserves judgement on *Pulp Fiction*.

## PICTURE CREDITS

The images in this book are from the archives of The Kobal Collection which owes its existence to the vision, talent and energy of the men and women who created the movie industry and whose legacies live on through the films they made, the studios they built, and the publicity photographs they took. Kobal collects, preserves, organizes and makes these images available to enhance our understanding of this cinematic art.

The publisher wishes to thank all of the photographers (known and unknown) and the film production and distribution companies whose publicity images appear in this book. We apologize in advance for any omissions, or neglect, and will be pleased to make any corrections in future editions.

20th Century Fox/Kobal/REX/Shutterstock: 15 left.

A Band Apart/Miramax/Kobal/REX/Shutterstock: 98, 99, 100, 101 above right, 103, 104, 106-107, 108, 109, 111, 112.

Andrew Cooper/Columbia/The Weinstein Company/Kobal/REX/Shutterstock: 155.

Andrew Cooper/The Weinstein Company/Kobal/REX/Shutterstock: 159 left, 159 right, 160 left, 160-161 right, 162-163 centre, 163 right, 164.

AP/REX/Shutterstock: 20 left.

BEI/REX/Shutterstock: 68.

Brc/Tesica/Kobal/REX/Shutterstock: 142.

Broadimage/REX/Shutterstock: 156.

CBS-TV/Kobal/REX/Shutterstock: 18 above right.

Claudio Onorati/Epa/REX/Shutterstock: 114.

Columbia/Kobal/REX/Shutterstock: 22, 82, 131, 166, 167, 168-169, 169 above right, 169 below right, 170-171.

Columbia/The Weinstein Company/Kobal/REX/Shutterstock: 143 above left, 143 below left, 143 right, 144, 145, 146-147 left, 149, 150, 151, 152-153, 154.

Darren Michaels/Miramax/A Band Apart/Kobal/REX/Shutterstock: 93.

Dimension Films/A Band Apart/Kobal/REX/Shutterstock: 115 below left, 115 right, 117, 118, 119, 120, 121, 123, 126, 127.

Dimension Films/Kobal/REX/Shutterstock: 115 above left.

Films Concorde/Kobal/REX/Shutterstock: 128.

Golden Harvest/Kobal/REX/Shutterstock: 17.

Granger/REX/Shutterstock: 165.

Ilpo Musto/REX/Shutterstock: 11, 81.

Joyce Podell/Los Hooligans/A Band Apart/Kobal/REX/Shutterstock: 61 right.

Kobal/REX/Shutterstock: 29 above right, 58.

Linda R. Chen/Live/Kobal/REX/Shutterstock: 41.

Linda R. Chen/Miramax/Buena Vista/Kobal/REX/Shutterstock: 8-9, 69, 74-75, 76 below.

Live Entertainment/Kobal/REX/Shutterstock: 6, 28, 29 above left, 29 below right, 29 below left, 35, 36, 37, 38-39, 40, 43, 64.

Los Hooligans/A Band Apart/Kobal/REX/Shutterstock: 59 right, 60, 61 left, 62-63.

Matt Baron/BEI/REX/Shutterstock: 23 left.

Miramax/A Band Apart/Kobal/REX/Shutterstock: 83 left, 96 above, 97.

Miramax/Buena Vista/Kobal/REX/Shutterstock: 4-5, 26, 30, 65, 66-67, 70, 72-73, 76 above, 77 above, 78-79.

Miramax/Kobal/REX/Shutterstock: 44, 80, 84, 89.

Morgan Creek/Davis/Kobal/REX/Shutterstock: 27, 47, 49 right, 51, 52 below.

Moviestore/REX/Shutterstock: 12, 13, 14, 15 below right, 16, 18 left, 18 below right, 20-21 centre, 33, 34, 42, 45, 53, 56 right, 59 left, 77 below, 83 right, 85, 86-87 right, 88, 89, 91, 94-95, 96 below, 101 below left, 101 below right, 102, 105, 113, 124, 147 right, 148, 157 below left, 158.

Moviestore Collection/REX/Shutterstock: 71.

Paramount/Kobal/REX/Shutterstock: 46 left, 46 right.

Paramount/Rafran/Kobal/REX/Shutterstock 21 right.

Ron Phillips/Morgan Creek/Davis/Kobal/REX/Shutterstock: 48-49, 50, 52 above.

Savoy/Kobal/REX/Shutterstock: 7, 90.

Shutterstock: 29 background.

Sidney Baldwin/Warner Bros/Kobal/REX/Shutterstock: 24-25, 55, 57.

SNAP/REX/Shutterstock: 10, 32, 54, 86.

Snap Stills/REX/Shutterstock: 92, 110, 116, 122-123, 123 right.

Steve Sands/AP/REX/Shutterstock: 23 right.

The Weinstein Company/Kobal/REX/Shutterstock: 157 above left, 157 right.

United Artists/Kobal/REX/Shutterstock: 19.

Universal/Kobal/REX/Shutterstock, 15 above right, 129, 130, 132, 133, 134, 135, 136, 137, 138-139, 140-141.

Universal/GTO/Kobal/REX/Shutterstock: 31 left, 31 right.

Warner Bros/Kobal/REX/Shutterstock: 56 left.